W9-AOT-959

WORLD HISTORY

The Relocation of the North American Indian

John M. Dunn

LUCENT BOOKS

An imprint of Thomson Gale, a part of The Thomson Corporation

THOMSON

™

GALE

Detroit • New York • San Francisco • San Diego • New Haven, Conn. • Waterville, Maine • London • Munich

LIBRARY OF CONGRESS CATALOGING-IN-PUBLICATION DATA

Dunn, John M., 1949–
    The relocation of the North American Indian / by John M. Dunn.
        p. cm. — (World history)
    Includes bibliographical references and index.
    ISBN 1-59018-656-7 (hard cover : alk. paper)
    1. Indians of North America—Relocation. 2. Indians of North America—Land tenure. 3. Indian reservations—North America. I. Title. II. Series: World history series.
E93.D864 2005
323.1197'073'09034—dc22
                                                                        2005001800

Printed in the United States of America

Contents

Foreword

Each year, on the first day of school, nearly every history teacher faces the task of explaining why his or her students should study history. Many reasons have been given. One is that lessons exist in the past from which contemporary society can benefit and learn. Another is that exploration of the past allows us to see the origins of our customs, ideas, and institutions. Concepts such as democracy, ethnic conflict, or even things as trivial as fashion or mores, have historical roots.

Reasons such as these impress few students, however. If anything, these explanations seem remote and dull to young minds. Yet history is anything but dull. And therein lies what is perhaps the most compelling reason for studying history: History is filled with great stories. The classic themes of literature and drama—love and sacrifice, hatred and revenge, injustice and betrayal, adversity and overcoming adversity—fill the pages of history books, feeding the imagination as well as any of the great works of fiction do.

The story of the Children's Crusade, for example, is one of the most tragic in history. In 1212 Crusader fever hit Europe. A call went out from the pope that all good Christians should journey to Jerusalem to drive out the hated Muslims and return the city to Christian control. Heeding the call, thousands of children made the journey. Parents bravely allowed many children to go, and entire communities were inspired by the faith of these small Crusaders. Unfortunately, many boarded ships captained by slave traders, who enthusiastically sold the children into slavery as soon as they arrived at their destination. Thousands died from disease, exposure, and starvation on the long march across Europe to the Mediterranean Sea. Others perished at sea.

Another story, from a modern and more familiar place, offers a soul-wrenching view of personal humiliation but also the ability to rise above it. Hatsuye Egami was one of 110,000 Japanese Americans sent to internment camps during World War II. "Since yesterday we Japanese have ceased to be human beings," he wrote in his diary. "We are numbers. We are no longer Egamis, but the number 23324. A tag with that number is on every trunk, suitcase and bag. Tags, also, on our breasts." Despite such dehumanizing treatment, most internees worked hard to control their bitterness. They created workable communities inside the camps and demonstrated again and again their loyalty as Americans.

These are but two of the many stories from history that can be found in the pages of the Lucent Books World History series. All World History titles rely on sound research and verifiable evidence, and all give students a clear sense of time, place, and chronology through maps and time-lines as well as text.

All titles include a wide range of author-itative perspectives that demonstrate the complexity of historical interpretation and sharpen the reader's critical thinking skills. Formally documented quotations and annotated bibliographies enable students to locate and evaluate sources, often instantaneously via the Internet, and serve as valuable tools for further research and debate.

Finally, Lucent's World History titles present rousing good stories, featuring vivid primary source quotations drawn from unique, sometimes obscure sources such as diaries, public records, and con-temporary chronicles. In this way, the voic-es of participants and witnesses as well as important biographers and historians bring the study of history to life. As we are caught up in the lives of others, we are reminded that we too are characters in the ongoing human saga, and we are better prepared for our own roles.

Important Dates at the Time

1512
Michelangelo completes his magnificent paintings on the Sistine Chapel ceiling.

1676
Antoni van Leeuwenhoek sees microorganisms under a microscope.

1803
President Thomas Jefferson authorizes the Louisiana Purchase.

1830
Congress adopts the Indian Removal Act.

| 1500 | 1600 | 1700 | 1800 | 1875 |

A.D.

1607
England settles Jamestown, its first permanent colony in North America.

1824
Congress creates the U.S. Bureau of Indian Affairs.

1869
The Suez Canal opens.

1720
China takes control of Tibet.

1492
Columbus arrives in the New World.

of the Indian Relocation

1890
The U.S. Army massacres Lakota Sioux at Wounded Knee, South Dakota.

1903
U.S. Supreme Court rules that Congress can break treaties with Indian tribes.

1946
Congress creates the Indian Claims Commission to decide land claims against the federal government.

1884
Major European powers partition Africa.

1900	1925	1950	1975	2000

1897
Indian Territory is officially incorporated into federal Oklahoma Territory.

1923
Time magazine begins publication.

1908
Jack Johnson becomes the first black world heavyweight boxing champion.

1876
Sioux and Cheyenne defeat the Seventh Cavalry in the Battle of the Little Big Horn.

1989
The Smithsonian is ordered to return Native American remains to tribal custody.

Introduction

A Clash of Two Worlds

The arrival of European explorers in North America in the fifteenth century A.D. put two worlds on a collision course. Though the newcomers boasted of discovering the New World, the natives they encountered most likely descended from nomadic people who arrived in North America at least ten thousand years earlier. At the time of these first encounters, anywhere from one to 18 million aborigines lived north of Mexico, comprising three hundred separate tribes that spoke nearly as many languages. The largest groups were concentrated along the California coast, in the Southwest, and in the forested regions and coastal plains east of the Mississippi River. Many North American Indians were nomadic or semi-nomadic hunters. Others, like the Cherokee and Creek in the Southeast, were sedentary farmers who lived in communal villages of log cabins or huts. Many tribes lived peaceably, while others raided neighboring Indians as a way of life. Blood feuds and warfare among North American tribes, in fact, were common long before whites ever arrived in the New World.

American Indians, however, also had much in common, no matter where they lived. They tended to live in bands, tribes, and confederations. Men and women usually married and raised children in family groups. Tribal elders commonly served as advisers, not authoritarian rulers. Most Native Americans believed in the supernatural, and worshipped and revered a universal god, the Great Spirit. The natural world was an integral part of both their everyday and spiritual lives. Nature represented a vast web of life that sustained them and commanded awe and respect; they had no desire to subdue it.

The European explorers came from the Old World—a civilization of rival states and absolute monarchs who ruled by self-proclaimed "divine rights," fierce competition for political and military superiority, relatively advanced technology (notably firearms and tools), and agriculture-based economies. Most Europeans proclaimed the Christian faith as the only true faith, dismissing all other belief systems as pagan or satanic. Unlike the native North Americans, most Europeans believed biblical injunctions that humans were God's steward on Earth, destined to achieve dominion over the natural world.

In addition, fifteenth-century Europeans were motivated by new and growing emphases on education, scientific inquiry, and exploration. They came to the New World with centuries-old legal codes and traditions, many of which dealt with land ownership. In the European view, individuals had a right to own their own personal piece of Earth and to derive wealth from

Native Americans held a profound reverence for nature as the source of all life-giving plants and animals, such as the buffalo hunted by these Plains Indians.

it. Moreover, European legal traditions proclaimed theories of property rights that advanced the idea that some people had superior rights to land than others. To most Native Americans such ideas were preposterous. Land was sacred, like air and water, and belonged to no one person. Tribes, not individuals, occupied land and used it for the benefit of all.

In addition to differing concepts of religion and property, Europeans had different languages, food, medicine, and dress. The two cultures had different concepts of marriage, punishment, justice, leadership, and time. Cultural conflict between Europeans and Native Americans was perhaps inevitable, but the root of conflict was economic. "Greed and avarice on the part of the whites—in other words, the almighty dollar," asserted experienced Indian fighter General George Crook in the late nineteenth century, "is at the bottom of nine-tenths of all our Indian troubles."[1]

From the earliest days fear and revenge motivated much killing. Both sides committed unconscionable atrocities; however, it was the Europeans, and later the Americans, who systematically removed and dispossessed Indians from their ancestral lands. That process involved the deaths of Native Americans by the hundreds of thousands through violence and disease, and the permanent confining of survivors to squalid reservations in an area equal to 2.3 percent of the continent they were once free to roam.

Chapter One

A Lust for Land

Christopher Columbus's historic voyage in 1492 spawned the greatest land rush in history. Though many Europeans followed the Italian explorer to the New World seeking gold, fur, and other resources, most wanted land for colonies, businesses, plantations, small farms, towns, and homes. Like most other Europeans of the fifteenth century, Columbus believed the act of discovery authorized the discoverer to claim the lands on behalf of the monarch who had sponsored the expedition.

Columbus had religious backing. Pope Alexander VI, believing that God's divine law called for establishing a Christian empire over the earth, presumed to have the right to grant sovereignty of any new lands not already owned by a Christian ruler to whomever he pleased. Christians accepted his assertion that "the Pope . . . has power not only over Christians, but also over all infidels [non-Christians]."[2] Columbus's report of new lands in the Western Hemisphere, therefore, gave the pope more territory over which to cast his authority.

In 1493 the pope exercised this power by officially dividing the as-yet unmapped New World between Spain and Portugal to avoid territorial disputes between the two nations. Portugal received what later became Brazil; the rest of the New World went to Spain. The native people of these lands, however, received no consideration.

The Spanish Impact

Spain sent other adventurers to the New World in search of riches, fame, and empire. Many abused the aboriginal people they encountered. Officially, the Spanish government and the church forbade the mistreatment of the people whom Columbus—believing he had landed in the vicinity of India—mistakenly called Indians. However, Spanish soldiers of fortune often considered natives as subhuman savages, if not devils, and treated them

In 1492 Christopher Columbus and his crew come ashore in the Bahamas as a group of curious natives observes. The discovery of the New World spurred the greatest land rush in history.

with extreme brutality. Although many Christian missionaries tried to protect Indians as well as convert them to Christianity, traders sold the native people as slaves and brutal colonists burned them.

Throughout the Americas, in fact, the Spanish conquistadors left a dark legacy of enslavement, torture, and murder. They burned villages, imprisoned Indians, and confiscated lands and untold riches, creating an empire in the New World that ranged from South America to Florida to California. By the end of the sixteenth century, conquest, starvation, and disease had reduced the total Native American population to about 1 million.

More European Nations Join the Land Rush

Other nations were not content to let Spain and Portugal dominate the discovery of new continents. Sweden, Denmark, Holland, France, Russia, and England had territorial plans of their own and paid little heed to the pope's division of the New World. By the sixteenth century, European scholars had developed the Christian concepts of discovery into a legal principle called sovereignty of the soil. According to those who subscribed to this idea, any Christian nation had the right to lay claim to newly discovered lands in the New World and subjugate any natives living in these areas.

Such was the case in 1608 when French explorer Samuel de Champlain established Quebec in New France (Canada) and, backed by the French government, claimed one-third of North America in the name of the French king. From Quebec the French expanded southward along the Mississippi River. Less interested than other Europeans in land rights, the French developed close ties with Native Americans and sought their help in developing a lucrative fur trade. They also hoped their diplomacy would earn them

Columbus Takes Possession of Caribbean Natives

In his journal, translated by Clement Markham, Christopher Columbus states his intention to present to the king of Spain some of the inhabitants of the Caribbean islands he had visited. The explorer expects the natives to be converted to Christianity and put to work as servants.

Thursday, 11th of October,
[The Indians] go as naked as when their mothers bore them. . . . All I saw were youths, none more than thirty years of age. They are very well made, with very handsome bodies, and very good countenances. Their hair is short and coarse, almost like the hairs of a horse's tail. They wear the hairs brought down to the eyebrows, except a few locks behind, which they wear long and never cut. They paint themselves black, and they are the color of the Canarians [Canary Islanders, who tended to have darker skin than mainland Spaniards], neither black nor white. Some paint themselves white, others red, and others of what color they find. . . . They neither carry nor know anything of arms, for I showed them swords, and they took them by the blade and cut themselves through ignorance. . . . They should be good servants and intelligent . . . and I believe that they would easily be made Christians. . . . I . . . will take . . . at the time of my departure, six natives for your Highness [the king of Spain].

European Arrivals in North America

Spanish explorers arrived to settle and conquer lands in the Caribbean, Florida, Mexico, and along the Pacific coast. France established colonies in Canada and then southward along the Mississippi River toward the Gulf of Mexico. The English first settled in Virginia and Massachusetts, eventually expanding their settlements to form thirteen colonies along the Atlantic coast. These and other European settlers felt they had the right to purchase or take lands from native people already living in those areas.

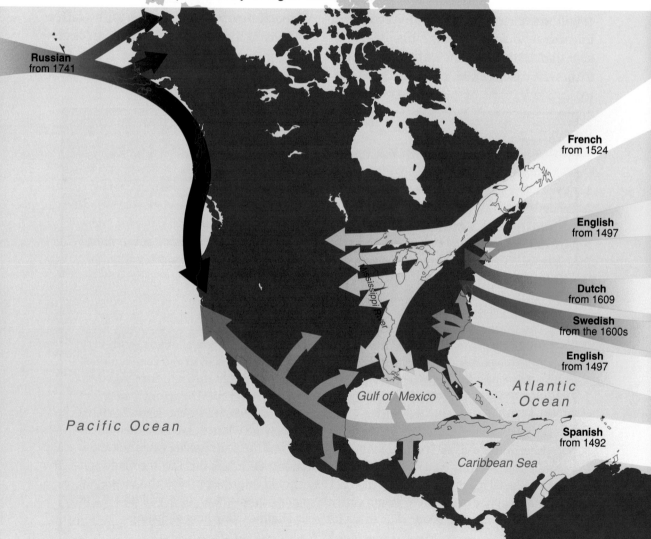

Russian
from 1741

French
from 1524

English
from 1497

Dutch
from 1609

Swedish
from the 1600s

English
from 1497

Spanish
from 1492

Pacific Ocean

Atlantic Ocean

Gulf of Mexico

Caribbean Sea

Mississippi River

the help of northeastern tribes such as the Abenaki, Algonquian, and Huron in repelling France's ancient European enemy, the English, who were also eagerly seeking new lands in North America.

The English Settlers

Like many other Europeans, the English justified taking lands in North America by invoking the principle of sovereignty of the soil. However, they adhered to a version of the legal theory that held that people already living on the lands in question still had a so-called right of occupancy. This right, according to European legal experts, was transferable to others by purchase or conquest. With these principles in mind, the English systematically displaced Indians beginning with the first permanent English colony at Jamestown, Virginia, in 1607. Relations quickly grew tense between the English and the confederacy of Algonquian tribes led by Chief Powhatan that dwelled in the Chesapeake Bay region. Many colonists were shocked by the physical appearance of these Native Americans and considered them savages. Wrote Captain John Smith, leader of Jamestown, of local natives in 1609:

> Their women some have their legs, hands, breasts and faces cunningly embroidered with diverse works, as beasts, serpents, artificially wrought into their flesh with black spots. In each ear commonly they have three great holes where at they hang chains, bracelets, or copper. Some of their men wear in those holes a small green and yellow colored snake, near half a yard in length, which crawling and lapping herself about his neck often times familiarly would kiss his lips. Others wear a dead rat tied by the tail.[3]

The Powhatan alliance, under its primary chief Openchancanough following Powhatan's death in 1618, feared and distrusted the heavily armed white newcomers. In 1622 hostilities broke out between the two groups when servants of a Jamestown planter, who had died at the hands of the Indians, killed an important Indian leader in retaliation. Powhatan warriors launched a general attack, killing 347 settlers in a few hours.

The English struck back, trying to exterminate the Indians. "It is infinitely better to have no heathen among us, who were but thorns in our sides, than to be at peace and league with them,"[4] declared the Virginia settlement's governor, Francis Wyatt.

Though the colony's financial backers feared that bloodshed could lead to instability and hostilities that would hamper colonial efforts, sporadic fighting continued for twenty years. The English had superior weapons and, eventually, superior numbers. By 1646 the Jamestown colonists had defeated the confederacy, confiscated their land, destroyed their villages, and forced survivors to live in restricted areas. This roundup foreshadowed the pattern that whites would use to control Indians in the coming years. The idea of Indian reservations was born in 1656 when Virginia and other English colonies first spoke of setting up certain areas exclusively for Indian use.

Conflict in Massachusetts

Troubles also brewed in the Northeast at the Plymouth colony, founded by English Pilgrims. In 1620 members of this separatist religious sect set sail from England headed for Virginia, but strong winds blew them far off course to Plymouth Rock, Massachusetts, where they decided to settle.

In 1625 some of the newcomers asked Samoset, a local chief of the Wampanoag, to give them 12,000 acres (48.6 sq. km) of land. Their request amused the Indian leader, who like most other Native Americans, believed no individual could own land. "To humor these strangers in their strange ways," writes author Dee Brown, "he went through a ceremony of transferring the land and made his mark on a paper for them. It was the first deed of Indian land to English colonists."[5]

But amusement turned to anger and hostility when more colonists arrived, established more New England settlements, and took land without asking. When Indians objected to the clearing of forests and the building of houses and

Chief Samoset of the Wampanoag makes a gesture of welcome to Pilgrim colonists, hard at work clearing land for their settlement at Plymouth.

other buildings, Governor John Winthrop of the Puritan Massachusetts Bay Colony, founded in 1629–1630, responded that colonists were merely filling a vacuum in the wilderness. Besides, he said, Indians had not tamed the lands they lived on and therefore had no legal right to them—to the Puritans, improvement and development was the logical basis of property rights.

Increased Puritan Demands

Like the Spaniards before them, the Puritans also interpreted their encounters with Indians in religious terms. The wilderness was not merely uncultivated land; it was the wild land of devils. Many English, in fact, firmly believed that Satan dwelled in untamed America to escape the advance of Christianity, and that Indians were agents of the devil whose purpose was to tempt and destroy the Europeans. Historian Gary Wills explains that the Puritans were convinced that the Indians were satanic, going so far as to think that "even friendly overtures [from Indians] were likely to be part of a larger strategy to disarm Christians."[6] Such attitudes led many Puritans to view their mission in America as a religious battle against the powers of darkness and evil represented by Native Americans.

Bay Colony War

Tensions between Indians and the English settlers in Massachusetts exploded in 1637 when Indians killed an English sea captain who had kidnapped a group of local Pequot and tried to sell them as slaves. Colonists retaliated on May 26 by slaugh-

In 1676 an Indian ally of the colonists fires on Wampanoag chief King Philip in a swamp.

tering Indian men, women, and children and burning wigwams full of sleeping people. "It is supposed that no less than five or six hundred [Pequot] souls were brought down to hell that day,"[7] wrote leading Puritan minister Cotton Mather. The victorious whites enjoyed almost forty years without full-scale hostilities until 1675, when a Wampanoag leader named Metacomet, whom the settlers called King Philip, forged an alliance among regional tribes to halt English encroachment of

Indian lands. The bloody fighting known as King Philip's War ensued and lasted until one August night in 1676, when Massachusetts and Connecticut troops tracked Philip down in a swamp, where he was shot by an Indian ally of the whites. Soldiers then quartered the Indian leader, severed his head, and placed it in the Fort Hill Tower, where his skull remained for twenty-five years, its eye sockets serving as nests for birds, as a symbol of broken Indian power.

Colonists also meted out severe punishment to Philip's defeated forces. They sold many, including Philip's wife and young children, into slavery in the West Indies and forced others to move onto nearby farms run and owned by white overseers.

King Philip's uprising inspired such widespread fear and hatred throughout New England that many colonists turned against all Indians, even friendly native tribes such as the Mohegan and the Pequot, and forced them off their lands.

Native American Tribal Homelands

Native tribes populated all areas of North America prior to the Europeans' arrival. Original homelands of some of the major tribes are shown on the map below. Since Indians did not believe in individual ownership of land, they did not always understand the consequences of making land agreements or treaties with white settlers.

(Modern boundaries shown for reference)

A Pattern of War and Removal

Numerous other brutal and bloody engagements between the English and the Indians occurred along the eastern seaboard from Georgia to New England during the 1600s. The outcome of the conflicts was ultimately the same: Indians were subdued, annihilated, enslaved, or driven away as English settlers occupied their lands and moved inland, searching for more territory, and as Indians could not maintain a united opposition. By now, many English argued that by right of discovery all North America belonged to the English king—and only the king, not Indians, could grant land titles.

In London, however, government officials disapproved of the growing violence settlers used against Indians. To placate Native Americans and prevent more bloodshed, the officials developed a new colonial policy that required whites to recognize the Indians' right of occupancy and to compensate them for any land that was taken. The New World settlers, however, lived far from the authority of the Crown and Parliament and generally did as they pleased.

English Rationale for Land Confiscation

As English colonists relentlessly confiscated Indian lands, many tried to justify their actions with new arguments. By the late seventeenth century many English agreed with European philosophers who argued that land was intended by God to be used efficiently and productively by humans to produce for the common good and to produce the greatest "revenue." That is, those individuals willing to make the best use of land had a natural right to take possession of it. Advocates of this position claimed that American Indians, who hunted for their livelihood, did not use the land as efficiently as Europeans who farmed. Moreover, nomadic native tribes had no right of occupancy to wilderness areas because they never stayed long in one place. An English observer once opined that the Powhatan had "no particular property in any part or parcel of the country, but only a general residencie there, as wild beasts have in the forest."[8]

According to eighteenth-century Swiss jurist Emmerich von Vattel, because "savages stood in no particular need [of land], and of which they made no actual and constant use, [Europeans] were lawfully entitled to take possession of it, and settle it with colonies."[9] The English, like many other Europeans, also believed that an individual had the right to own a parcel of land.

But such thinking mystified Native Americans. How could anyone possess a piece of Earth? Land was like air, streams, the clouds, something the Great Spirit, or God, had blessed the Earth with for all to use. When Indians spoke of their lands, they usually meant a place for their tribe to occupy temporarily, not for individuals and their heirs to possess forever.

Understandably, such differing concepts created misunderstanding when the English negotiated land transfers from Indians. Sometimes, whites struck deals with individual Indians who lacked authority to speak or negotiate for an entire tribe. Because most Native Americans could not read or speak English and did

Who Best Uses the Land?

Many of the first Europeans in North America were convinced that because they farmed more efficiently—that is, produced higher yields from the land—they had a greater right to the land than Indians. The British financial backers of the Virginian colony made this point in a passage from The Records of the Virginia Company of London, *vol.3, edited by Susan Kingsbury.*

For the land, being tilled and used well by us, deceive not our expectation but rather exceeded it far, being so thankful as to return a hundred for one. But the savages, though never a nation . . . have instead of that harvest which our pains merited, returned nothing but briars and thorns, pricking even to death many of their bene-factors. Yet doubt we not, but that as all wickedness is crafty to undo itself, so these also have more wounded themselves than us, God Almighty making way for sever-ity there, where a fair gentleness would not take place.

not understand oral explanations of complex legal contracts written by whites, they often signed away all property rights when they had intended only to allow occupancy, travel, or hunting rights. The English, of course, insisted that signed contracts or treaties gave them the legal right to take full, permanent possession of the land. Complicating matters was the fact that the land boundaries set by the English were often generally defined and subject to alteration.

Some historians and writers believe that relentless white encroachment on Indian lands and the resulting relocation of the Native Americans who lived there was inevitable, and that prevention of bloody clashes was almost impossible. "Whites cannot be severely blamed for trespassing upon what was called Indians' land. . . . The man who puts the soil to use must of right dispossess the man who does not, or the world will come to a standstill. . . . On the border [frontier] each man was a law unto himself, and good and bad alike were left in perfect freedom to [do what he wanted] almost without . . . hinderance,"[10] wrote Theodore Roosevelt, the twenty-sixth president of the United States, in his multivolume history *The Winning of the West.*

Other observers cannot justify the conflict. "Behind the English invasion of North America," writes contemporary historian and social critic Howard Zinn, "behind their massacre of Indians, their deception, their brutality, was that special powerful drive born in civilizations based on private property. . . . The need for space, for land, was a real human need. But in conditions of scarcity . . . this human need was transformed into the murder of whole peoples."[11]

Chapter Two

Colonial Struggles for Control

By the late 1600s England and France were struggling for dominance in North America. Meanwhile, continued immigration from Britain swelled the English colonies. By 1740 over 1.5 million English had arrived, making them the biggest European group in North America. Their growing numbers also caused crowding in the colonies and spurred the demand for new lands to the west.

However, a natural border made western expansion difficult. The Appalachian Mountains, which run north to south for over 2,000 miles (3,200 km) from Georgia to Maine, kept the growing colonial population penned between the Atlantic coast and mountain foothills. Gradually increasing numbers of land-hungry settlers nevertheless found passages through the Appalachian highlands and moved into uncharted lands where Native Americans had lived for centuries.

Trouble awaited them, for the French had long lived and traded in this region.

Now the territorial goals of the nations were in conflict. The French wanted to keep the British out of the Ohio Valley, a fertile region that lay west of the Appalachians. The English, though, desired this territory, plus all of French-held Canada.

Two Sides Collide

As the two sides collided, both the British and French enlisted various Indian tribes as allies who mistakenly believed their grateful European partners would protect their hunting lands from encroachment. The Europeans, however, were primarily interested in using Indians as pawns in their battle with each other.

Wrote a French missionary in Nova Scotia, Abbé Jean-Louis Le Loutre, to a French government minister: "My plan is to persuade the Indians to send word to the English that they will not permit new settlements to be made in Acadia [the name of the French colony. . . . I shall do my best to make it look to the English as

This eighteenth-century painting depicts a regiment of French troops, aided by colonial and North American allies, firing on the British during the French and Indian War.

if this plan comes from the Indians and that I have no part of it."[12]

Rivalry between England and France resulted in repeated clashes from the late 1600s until well past the mid-1700s. The English named the last major episode in this ongoing battle—a fight for control of the Ohio Valley beginning in 1756—the French and Indian War. As whites killed one other, some Indian leaders suspected that Native Americans ultimately had the most at stake. "Why do not you and the French fight in the old country and the sea?" Shingas, the Delaware chief, asked

the British in 1758. "Why do you come to fight on our land? This makes everybody believe you want to take the land from us by force and settle it."[13]

After several defeats during the early stages of the French and Indian War, the British triumphed in 1763. In accordance with the Treaty of Paris, signed on February 10, 1763, France ceded Canada and all its land claims east of the Mississippi River except for New Orleans. At about the same time, Spain ceded Florida to England. Together, these land cessions meant that England claimed control of virtually the entire eastern half of North America. With this incentive, English-speaking settlers migrated farther west. By doing so they helped fulfill Pennsylvanian Benjamin Franklin's prediction that one day "all the country from the St. Lawrence to the Mississippi will in another century be filled with British people."[14]

Alarm Spreads Through the Ohio Valley

France's former Indian allies along the Great Lakes and the Ohio River grew fearful and anguished as English newcomers swarmed into the conquered areas, confiscated Indian lands, and punished the tribes that had sided with France. Soon, English and colonial land investment companies also moved into the region. One of them—the Ohio Company—was granted 200,000 acres (809 sq. km) of land along the Upper Ohio River by the British government. Another grant deeded another company, owned by George Washington and other leading colonists, 2.5 million acres (10,100 sq. km) in the Mississippi Valley territory to sell to settlers.

A Colonial City Announces a Shocking Policy

The history of the removal of the North American Indian is filled with accounts of extremely harsh treatment of Native Americans who resisted the authority of whites. In this 1755 proclamation cited in Vine Deloria Jr.'s Custer Died for Your Sins, *an official in colonial Boston declares a policy of genocide against the Penobscot tribe and announces a schedule of brutalities.*

Whereas the tribe of Penobscot Indians have repeatedly in a perfidious [deceitful] manner acted contrary to their solemn submission unto his Majesty long since made and frequently renewed.

I . . . therefore . . . declare the Penobscot Tribe of Indians to be enemies, rebels and traitors to his Majesty.

. . . And I do hereby require his Majesty's subjects of the Province to embrace all opportunities of pursuing, captivating, killing and destroy[ing] all and every of the aforesaid Indians.

And whereas the General Court of this Province have voted that a bounty . . . be granted and allowed to be paid out of the Province Treasury . . . the premiums of bounty following viz:

For every scalp of a male Indian brought in as evidence of their being killed as aforesaid, forty pounds. For every scalp of such female Indian or male Indian under the age of twelve years that shall be killed and brought in as evidence of their being killed as aforesaid, twenty pounds.

Ottawa chief Pontiac holds up a wampum belt as he tells his council of his plan to resist the encroachment of whites on native lands.

During this influx of whites, an Indian mystic named Neolin, known as the Delaware Prophet, proclaimed that the Great Spirit wanted him to warn Indians of a coming disaster. "I give you warning," he cried, "that if you suffer the Englishmen to dwell in your midst, their diseases and their poisons shall destroy you . . . and you shall die."[15]

Influenced by these words, the powerful Ottawa chief Pontiac organized an uprising in May 1763, imploring the Miami, Ottawa, Chippewa, Wyandot, Potawatomi, Delaware, and other tribes to combine forces. Pontiac's messengers delivered orders to these tribes to halt the white land grab, and attack nearby white settlements and forts. "Why, says the Great Spirit, do you suffer these dogs in red clothing [British soldiers] to enter your country and take the land I have given you?" Pontiac is said to have exclaimed. "Drive them from it! Drive them! When you are in distress I will help you!"[16] Pontiac, however, knew that his warriors could not actually force the more powerful and numerous English out of Ohio and the Great Lakes. Instead, he hoped to help restore the French to power so that they could accomplish this task. In late May, Pontiac's forces attacked the fortified community of Detroit, only recently vacated by the French, causing terror along the border outposts of Pennsylvania, Maryland, and Virginia. Slowly, Pontiac's warriors along with those of allied tribes pushed the English settlers back east toward the Alleghenies, the western ranges of the Appalachians, killing nearly two thousand whites. "I mean to destroy the English and leave not one upon our lands,"[17] promised the Ottawa leader.

Colonial responses to this insurrection—Pontiac's Rebellion—ranged from outrage to indifference. The rebellion did not affect colonists and authorities in the East, who gave the matter little attention beyond producing a rash of anti-Indian speeches. In fact, no colony provided aid to British troops. British armies did mount an offensive campaign beginning in 1764, and reinforced frontier garrisons to protect terrorized settlements.

Pontiac failed in the end. No French aid ever materialized. He was also unable to merge many different tribes into an effective fighting force for any sustained length of time. By 1766 the British had forced Pontiac to sue for peace, and the rebellion ended by treaty. A military failure for the Native Americans, Pontiac's Rebellion nevertheless caused shock waves of concern felt as far away as England.

A New British Policy

Startled by the ferocity of these Indian attacks, the British authorities felt compelled to act. The result was a document called the Proclamation of 1763, which the king and Parliament hoped would prevent future clashes. The proclamation established a north-to-south boundary line that followed the crest of the Appalachian Mountains, ranging from northern Georgia to Maine. English settlement was prohibited west of the line, a region including the Ohio Valley and the Great Lakes (also known as the Northwest Territory) inhabited by the Ottawa, Chippewa, Shawnee, and other tribes, unless official negotiations with Indians permitted such settlement.

The proclamation recognized Indian tribes as independent nations whose consent must be obtained to any proposed land sale or exchange of properties. Moreover, no longer could any individual British citizens deal with Indians for purposes of acquiring land. Only men designated as Indian agents, acting on behalf of the government in London, were so authorized.

On paper, at least, the Proclamation of 1763 was good news for American Indians living west of the Appalachians. It even included an acknowledgement that "great frauds and abuses have been committed in the purchasing land of the Indians, to the great prejudice of our [English] interests, and to the great dissatisfaction of the . . . Indians."[18]

The proclamation, however, was scorned by settlers who simply ignored the imaginary line and rushed westward into Indian-occupied territory. Many of these trespassers justified taking land in the forbidden zone by citing what they considered to be legal means. Some, for example, purchased documents called land warrants at low prices from British soldiers who had received them from the British government prior to the proclamation as payment for military services rendered in the Northwest Territory. The new owners of the warrants believed they were entitled to specified amounts of land and went west to claim them. Thousands of other settlers, meanwhile, also drove their wagons deep into Kentucky and western Pennsylvania in defiance of the proclamation and Indian protests.

Alarmed by the influx of whites, members of the Delaware and Shawnee tribes met with colonial representatives of New Jersey, Virginia, and Pennsylvania at Fort Stanwix, New York, in 1768 to reach a peaceful solution. Native Americans hoped to appease whites by agreeing to accept a new boundary line for Indian lands farther to the west: the Ohio River. Similar treaties negotiated with the Cherokee in 1768 at Hard Labor and in 1770 at Lochaber in present-day West Virginia both pushed the southern portions of the proclamation line farther west. Large numbers of migrating whites ignored these treaties as well. They brazen-

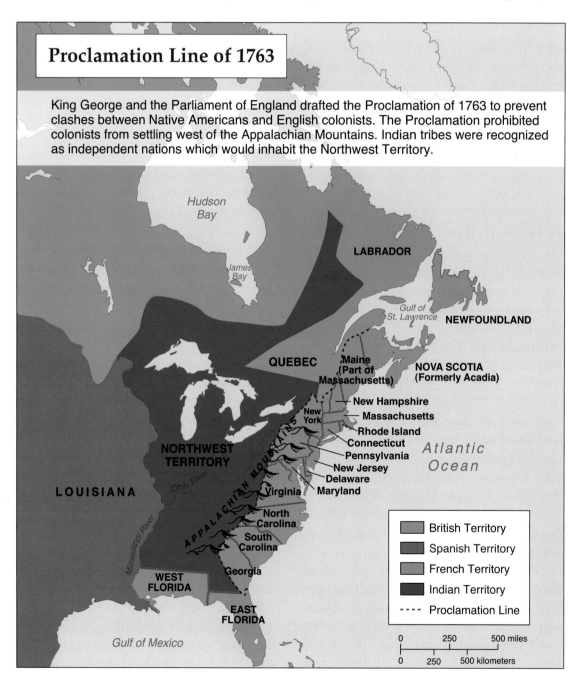

Proclamation Line of 1763

King George and the Parliament of England drafted the Proclamation of 1763 to prevent clashes between Native Americans and English colonists. The Proclamation prohibited colonists from settling west of the Appalachian Mountains. Indian tribes were recognized as independent nations which would inhabit the Northwest Territory.

Hudson Bay

James Bay

LABRADOR

Gulf of St. Lawrence   NEWFOUNDLAND

QUEBEC   Maine (Part of Massachusetts)

NOVA SCOTIA (Formerly Acadia)

New Hampshire
New York   Massachusetts
Rhode Island
Connecticut
Pennsylvania
New Jersey
Delaware
Virginia   Maryland

NORTHWEST TERRITORY

Atlantic Ocean

Ohio River

LOUISIANA

APPALACHIAN MOUNTAINS

North Carolina
South Carolina

Mississippi River

Georgia

WEST FLORIDA

EAST FLORIDA

Gulf of Mexico

British Territory
Spanish Territory
French Territory
Indian Territory
- - - Proclamation Line

0   250   500 miles
0   250   500 kilometers

The Proclamation of 1763 Offers Protection of Indian Lands

Although pioneering Americans ignored the Proclamation of 1763, Native Americans west of the Appalachians were temporarily hopeful that the document would halt colonial expansion. This excerpt is taken from Henry S. Commager's Documents of American History:

And whereas it is just and reasonable, and essential to our interest and the security of our [English] colonies, that the several nations or tribes of Indians with whom we are connected, and who live under our protection, should not be molested or disturbed in the possession of such parts of our dominions and territories, not having been ceded to or purchased by us, are reserved to them, . . . as their hunting-grounds. We do hereby strictly forbid . . . all our living subjects from making any purchases or settlements whatever, or taking possession of any of the [land reserved for Indians] without our special [permission]. . . .

And we do further strictly . . . require all [colonists who have settled on Indian lands] to remove themselves from such settlements. . . .

We . . . enjoin and require, that no private person do presume to make any purchase from the said Indians of any lands reserved to the said Indians.

ly crossed the Ohio River and the new southern borders, clashed violently with Indians, and staked land claims on Indian territories.

"Everywhere on the frontier is found new encroachment by our people as cabins are being built on Indian lands beyond the established white limitations," wrote William Johnson, a British Indian agent in 1774 to the Lords of Trade, a committee of British aristocrats charged with formulating colonial policy. "Worse, they abuse and maltreat the Indians at every meeting. It seems as if the people are determined to bring a new war, though their own ruin may be the consequence."[19]

Settlers saw the situation differently. British attempts to stop their advances into Indian lands struck them as unfair and indefensible. "The [American colonists] do not conceive that Government has any right to forbid their taking possession of a vast tract of country either uninhabited or which serves only as a shelter to a few scattered tribes of Indians,"[20] wrote Lord Dunmore, governor of Virginia, in 1774. In fact, colonists' lingering resentment of the Proclamation of 1763 helped ignite the American Revolution: Soon the biggest threat to Native Americans would be the government of the United States, not Britain.

Chapter Three

U.S. Expansion: An Era of Broken Treaties

When American colonialists revolted against England in 1775, Indians in the Ohio River Valley realized that their own fate depended on which nation won the war. Despite their distrust of the English, many tribes viewed the British as the lesser of two evils and threw them their support. The decision caused widespread regret later, when the Americans defeated the British and showed little sympathy for those who had opposed them.

Cooperation with the American colonists, however, gained the Native Americans little. For example, in 1778, U.S. officials negotiated a peace treaty with the Delaware—the first U.S.-Indian treaty—that allowed the Continental Army to pass through tribal territory to reach British forts. Tribal leaders also promised to aid the Americans against the British. In return, the Americans offered "any other tribes who have been friends to the interest of the United States, to join the present confederation, and to

form a state whereof the Delaware nation shall be the head, and have a representation in Congress."[21] It was a promise never kept.

Even more damaging to the Delaware was the fact that the treaty omitted any specific description of the boundaries of Delaware territory. This omission would affect almost all American Indians: It created a precedent that was followed in many future land negotiations and policies.

The peace treaty that ended the American Revolution in 1783 recognized specific boundaries for the newly formed United States: Canada to the north, the Mississippi River to the west, Florida—a territory that had slipped back into Spanish hands and ranged to the Mississippi River—and the Atlantic Ocean to the south and east, respectively.

The new American government now gave itself the authority to define the status of Indian lands within its borders. Because Britain had ceded all land rights associated with the territory, American officials felt free to void all land titles obtained by Indians during past dealings with the French and British. The United States also took a trustee position: Although the ultimate title now rested with the federal government, Indians did have a right to "occupy" the lands they currently lived on.

Meanwhile, the individual state governments retained the right to deal with Indians within their own borders, while the federal government assumed jurisdiction over all tribes living in the unorganized lands west of the Appalachians to the Mississippi River. Thus, the stage was set for further American encroachment on Indian lands.

Opening Up the Northwest to Settlement

Multitudes of Americans soon pressured their new government to open up Indian lands for settlement, especially in the lands

In 1682 William Penn presents a treaty to Delaware chiefs that ceded land to the Quakers. Nearly one hundred years later, U.S. officials negotiated another land-rights treaty with the Delaware.

A White View of Indian Warriors

James Smith was a white explorer, pioneer, woodsman, military officer, and settler who as a child had been adopted and reared by an Indian family on Pennsylvania's western frontier. From them he learned the ways of the Indian, including methods of warfare, in which he trained American fighters during the American Revolution. In 1799 he described these tactics in a book about his life, which is excerpted in Voices from the Wilderness, *edited by Thomas Froncek.*

I have often heard the British officers call the Indians the undisciplined savages, which is a capital mistake—as they have all the essentials of discipline. They are under good command, and punctual in obeying orders: they can act in concert, and when their officers lay a plan and give orders, they will cheerfully unite in putting all their directions into immediate execution. . . . When they go into battle they are not loaded or encumbered with many clothes, as they commonly fight naked, save only breech clout, leggins and mockesons. There is no such thing as corporeal punishment used, in order to bring them under such good discipline: degrading is the only chastisement, and they are so unanimous in this, that it effectually answers the purpose. Their officers plan, order and conduct matters until they are brought into action, and then each man is to fight as though he was to gain the battle himself. General orders are commonly given in time of battle, either to advance or retreat, and is done by a shout or yell, which is well understood, and then they retreat or advance in concert. They are generally well equipped, and exceeding expert and active in the use of arms. . . .

They train up their boys to the art of war from the time they are twelve or fourteen years of age. . . . [B]ut were only part of our men taught this art, accompanied with our continental discipline, I think no European power . . . would venture to shew its head in the American woods.

north of the Ohio River unofficially called the Northwest Territory, which eventually became the states of Indiana, Michigan, Ohio, Illinois, and Wisconsin.

Congress responded by passing the Land Ordinance of 1785, which carved up the territory into townships. Two years later, the lawmakers passed the Northwest Ordinance of 1787, which officially established the Northwest Territory and set the conditions for settling in the area. The new law also addressed the rights of the Indians living in this region: "The utmost good faith shall always be observed towards the Indians; their lands and property shall never be taken from them without their consent; and in their property, rights, and liberty, they shall never be invaded or disturbed, unless in just and lawful wars authorized by Congress."[22]

Such official assurance, however, proved false; squatters, settlers, trappers, and adventurers poured into the Indian lands, nearly unimpeded by the U.S. government. Their arrival enraged Indian tribes living in the region, such as the Shawnee, Miami, Potawatomi, and Chippewa, and in 1790 many of their warriors followed Miami Chief Little Turtle in a violent effort to expel the intruders.

When President George Washington learned the Miami Confederacy was going to war, he approved an attack on the main Miami settlement of Kekionga, near present-day Fort Wayne, Indiana. Little Turtle's forces ambushed and defeated this army, and another a year later, in the worst defeats of an American army by Native American forces. Finally, however, the Miami Confederacy surrendered in 1794, and in 1795 the Indians signed the Treaty of Greenville, a document that ceded to the United States most of present-day central and southern Ohio and parts of Indiana. The treaty also stated that Americans could purchase, when they pleased, the remainder of Indian lands east of the Mississippi and north of the Ohio River.

By now, in compliance with their negotiated settlement with the Americans, the British had removed all their troops from the Northwest Territory to Canada. Without their ally Indians halted their resistance and American settlers resumed occupying lands in the Ohio Valley. By

During the late 1700s, trappers and settlers flocked to the Northwest Territory, previously specified as Indian Land.

1800 roughly 1 million whites lived between the Mississippi River and the Appalachian Mountains, the landmark that served as the Westernmost border of European settlement only thirty-seven years previously. In 1801 new legislation divided the Northwest Territory into the Northwest and Indiana Territories, whose administrators aggressively sought title to Indian lands. The Indian tribes had fewer and fewer places to go.

Demanding a New Home for Indians in Louisiana

In 1803 U.S. president Thomas Jefferson made the biggest real estate deal in history when he paid France $15 million for 829,000 square miles (2.15 million sq. km) of North America called the Louisiana Territory. With this purchase Jefferson doubled the area of the United States. For four cents an acre, he added lands to the United

Relocating Indian Tribes West of the Mississippi

One year after purchasing the Louisiana Territory—roughly one-third of the continental United States—from France in 1803, the federal government announced an exchange-of-land policy that moved Indians east of the Mississippi into the newly acquired region. The precedent-setting proclamation of March 26, 1804, is excerpted in John Upton Terrell's book Land Grab: The Truth About "The Winning of the West."

The President of the United States is hereby authorized to stipulate with any Indian tribes owning lands on the East side of the Mississippi, and residing thereon, for an exchange of lands the property of the United States, on the West side of the Mississippi, in case the said tribe shall remove and settle thereon: but, in such stipulation the said tribes shall acknowledge themselves to be under the protection of the United States, and shall agree that they will not hold any treaty with any foreign Power, individual State, or with the individuals of any State or Power; and that they will not sell and dispose of the said lands, or any part thereof, to any sovereign Power, except the United States, nor to the subjects or citizens of any other sovereign Power, nor to the citizens of the United States.

States that later became the states of Louisiana, Arkansas, Oklahoma, Missouri, North and South Dakota, Iowa, Nebraska, Kansas, Minnesota, Colorado, Wyoming, and Montana. The Mississippi River was also part of the package.

One of Jefferson's several reasons for negotiating the purchase was to broaden his options in handling Native Americans in the Northwest and Indiana Territories. Earlier in his life he had championed land rights of Indians. As white Americans moved west, however, Jefferson's views hardened against the people he once vowed to protect. He now wrote: "We shall be obliged to drive them [the Indians] with the beasts of the forest into the stony mountains."[23]

Soon American officials pressured tribal chiefs to relocate, as Jefferson wished. Browbeaten, outnumbered, and unable to prevent aggressive white settlement, various tribes concluded they had little choice, short of war, but to comply with U.S. treaty makers and exchange their lands for money, food, supplies, and the promise of new homes west of the Mississippi.

The Rise of Tecumseh

One of the principal treaty negotiators for the Americans was William Henry Harrison, superintendent of the Northwest Indians and governor of Indiana Territory from 1801 to 1813. Like many other whites at the time, Harrison disdained Indians. "Is one of the fairest portions of the globe to remain in a

William Henry Harrison trots his horse over a fallen Indian warrior during the Battle of Tippecanoe in 1811. Throughout his life, Harrison exhibited a great disdain for Indians.

state of nature, the haunt of a few wretched savages," he exclaimed before the territorial legislature in 1810, "when it seems destined, by the Creator, to give support to a large population, and to be the seat of civilization, of science, and true religion?"[24]

With this mindset, Harrison took control of vast areas of Indian lands by negotiating (sometimes, say his critics, by stealth and deceit) fifteen separate treaties that collectively required Indians to hand over a huge part of present-day Ohio, the rest of Indiana, Illinois, and sections of Wisconsin and Michigan, all for about a penny per acre.

His actions sparked an angry response from a charismatic Shawnee chief named Tecumseh. "Sell a country!" thundered Tecumseh. "Why not sell the air, the cloud and the great sea?"[25]

Shawnee chief Tecumseh built a confederacy of Indians east of the Mississippi in an effort to halt the white invasion of Indian lands.

Tecumseh, a veteran of Little Turtle's uprising, was an eloquent speaker and a strong, smart leader, respected by both Indians and whites. Even Tecumseh's avowed enemy Harrison praised the leader: "He is one of those uncommon geniuses which spring up occasionally to produce revolutions and overturn the established order of things."[26]

Although neither Jefferson nor the next three American presidents used military force to remove Indians, Tecumseh and other chiefs distrusted treaties and believed that eventually the Americans would forcibly oust their tribes from their ancestral lands and send them west. Tecumseh's distrust stemmed from personal experience, and his strategy, while designed to benefit all Indians, was also based on a personal desire for revenge. He never forgot that white settlers killed his father and an older brother when they fought to prevent intruders from seizing Indian land. He had refused to sign the Treaty of Greenville in 1745, and set out to create a vast confederacy of all Indians east of the Mississippi, vowing to halt the white invasion of Indian lands.

With his brother, a powerful orator known as the Prophet, Tecumseh traveled from Florida to the Canadian Great Lakes, imploring other Native Americans to unite against the corrupting influence of white culture and power, reject invalid treaties, and adhere to traditional ways. "The way, the only way to stop this evil," he exhorted, "is for the red men to unite in claiming a common and equal right in the land, as it was at first, and should be now—for it was never divided, but belonged to all."[27]

Tecumseh Calls for Resistance

White settlers poured into the Ohio Valley during the decades following the American Revolution and seized Indian land. Angered by this incursion, Shawnee chief Tecumseh called on his tribe to aid the British in halting the Americans. This excerpt from his eloquent plea appears in Witness to America, *edited by Stephen Ambrose and Douglas Brinkley.*

*L*isten! When war [was] declared, our father [the British king] stood up and gave us the tomahawk and told us that he was ready to strike the Americans; that he wanted our assistance; and that he would certainly get us our lands back, which the Americans had taken from us. . . .

Listen, Father! The Americans have not yet defeated us by land; neither are we sure that they have done so by water—we therefore wish to remain here and fight our enemy, should they make their appearance. If they defeat us, we will then retreat with our father. . . .

Father! You have got the arms and ammunition which our great father sent for his red children. If you have an idea of going away, give them to us, and you may go and welcome, for us. Our lives are in the hand of the Great Spirit. We are determined to defend our lands, and if it is His will, we wish to leave our bones upon them.

Harrison warily watched Tecumseh build a confederacy and resolved to destroy the Indian alliance before a general uprising. He got his chance in November 1811, while Tecumseh was away with his best warriors on a recruiting mission. On November 7 Harrison led one thousand men in an attack against Tecumseh's village, called Prophet's Town, on the Wabash River near Tippecanoe Creek, in Indiana. In heavy fighting, the Americans suffered 190 casualties but destroyed the village and scattered the surviving warriors, disrupting Tecumseh's dream of a unified Indian resistance. Indian raids continued to terrorize the frontier, but the confederacy faltered.

Tecumseh, though, had one last hope: an alliance with the English. "The Americans we must fight, not the English," he told his Indian allies. "The Americans are our eternal foes, the hungry devourers of the country of our fathers."[28]

Siding with the British

When the U.S. Congress convened in 1811, many representatives clamored for war against Britain. These "war hawks" came mainly from the western and southern regions of the United States, citing many grievances against their old enemy. Their immediate concerns were the British practices of intercepting and seizing neutral American merchant ships headed for

American soldiers fire on charging Indians near Tippecanoe Creek. After the battle, Tecumseh and his allies resolved to side with the British during the War of 1812.

France, which was at war with Britain, and British impressment, the kidnapping of thousands of American sailors and forced service in the British navy, on a pretext that they were British deserters. Many Americans were also convinced that the British were arming Indians in Canada to raid settlers in the United States. Many war hawks had territorial goals—the expansion of American borders. They saw war as a means of adding Canada and Florida to the growing American republic. For all

these reasons, America was catapulted into war against the British in 1812.

The British goal at the onset of the fighting was to keep the United States from expanding westward, a plan that dovetailed squarely with Tecumseh's mission. The British and Tecumseh's Indian forces joined to battle the Americans in the regions of Lake Erie and Lake Michigan.

The bloody fighting ended two years later, settling little between the Americans and the British but effectively crushing

Indian resistance in the region. In 1813 Harrison, now a general, defeated the British-Indian allies at the Battle of the Thames, killing Tecumseh. The great chief's dream died with him. "The real losers were the Indians," argues historian Rebecca Brooks Gruver. "After suffering heavy casualties, they no longer had any promise of British firearms or supplies. In effect, they were left to the mercy of the land-hungry American people."[29]

This collapse of Indian resistance meant an easier passage for the white settlers moving westward. Many of the latest migrants were unemployed workers who had lost their maritime jobs in the Northeast when the war disrupted commercial shipping. Improved steamboats, canals, and roads made it easier than ever before for whites to venture west.

The War of 1812 was also a turning point for the American people. Previously, many settlers were European-born immigrants who lacked a strong sense of loyalty to any state or the new national government. But now, "The war has renewed and reinstated the national feelings and character which the Revolution had given," observed Albert Gallatin, the U.S secretary of the treasury. "They are more Americans; they feel and act more as a nation."[30]

This new surge of national loyalty also prompted many Americans to turn to the federal government to cancel Indian titles to land in the Northwest and Indiana Territories and protect newly arrived settlers from Indian attacks. The federal government responded by sending official commissioners to negotiate with one remaining tribe after another to obtain their lands. Weakened and demoralized, the tribes complied with U.S. demands and moved farther west.

In the South, meanwhile, Native Americans also faced growing pressures to yield their lands. Soon, they too would face the full wrath and power of the federal government.

Chapter Four

Forced Removal from the East

As white settlers poured into the American Midwest, many government officials abandoned hopes of coexistence with Indians in the Ohio River Valley and instead openly advocated a policy of forced removal. As early as 1825, President James Monroe suggested the relocation of Native Americans west of the Mississippi River: "In their present state, it is impossible to incorporate them . . . into our system. . . . The great object . . . is the removal of those tribes."[31] Monroe argued that such a removal benefited both Americans and Indians: Whites would get the land they coveted, and the nation's natives would avoid "wars between them and the United States."[32]

What Monroe envisioned was the relocation of an estimated ninety-seven thousand Native Americans then living in North Carolina, Georgia, Alabama, Tennessee, Ohio, Indiana, Illinois, Missouri, New York, Arkansas, and Michigan. Although such a massive undertaking would prove costly, violate existing treaties protecting tribal land rights, and perhaps ignite bloody resistance, the idea of Indian removal gained popularity across the nation.

Support for the idea was especially strong in the South, where whites had long desired the homelands of the Cherokee, Chickasaw, Creek, Choctaw, and Seminole, collectively known as the Five Civilized Tribes because their cultures had such "civilized" features as sedentary, permanent communities; agriculture; and organized government. Despite these parallels with the practices of European Americans, many white leaders, including a famed Indian fighter named Andrew Jackson, demanded the removal of the southern tribes.

Opposite: This seventeenth-century engraving depicts a Native American corn farm in the Carolinas.

Southern Tribes Fight to Save Their Lands

When Jackson became president in 1829, many southern whites rejoiced; now there was a champion of Indian removal in the White House. By this time relations between whites and Native Americans were especially tense in Georgia, Alabama, and Mississippi, where state officials had not only outlawed tribal governments, but also confiscated large tracts of Indian land and opened them up to settlement. In Georgia, for instance, state officials gave away vast stretches of land to whites as lottery prizes. Mobs of settlers and speculators, encouraged or ignored by state officials, attacked Indians, sold them liquor, and bullied, bribed, and cheated them out of their lands.

Soon after Andrew Jackson was elected president in 1829, he signed the Indian Removal Act that forced all Indians to relocate west of the Mississippi River.

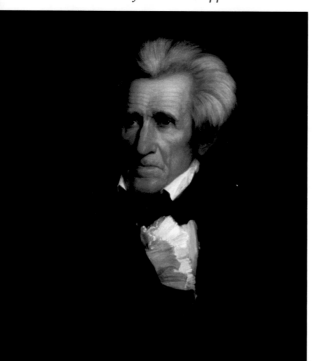

The clamor for Cherokee lands rose to a fever pitch in 1829, when gold was discovered in northern Georgia. As squatters and prospectors poured into these Appalachian highlands, Cherokee appealed to the federal government for protection. No assistance came, though the Indian Trade and Intercourse Act of 1802 stated that Indians could be dispossessed of their lands only by treaty. This law further stated that only the federal government had the authority to govern Indian affairs.

Federal power, however, was used to displace Indians. This process began in 1830 with a law that Jackson pushed through Congress called the Indian Removal Act. The act called for the relocation of all Indians—in the North as well as in the Southeast—to regions west of the Mississippi River. There they would receive new lands in exchange for those they abandoned, "guaranteed" to be theirs "forever." Indians who did not move west would become citizens of the state in which they resided. The law also promised relocated Indians protection against intruders in their new lands, and assured Indians that their new homes would never be incorporated into any state or territory.

Removal, insisted Jackson, was the best way to protect southern Indians from the assaults of land-hungry squatters and speculators. In addition, however, the president feared that independent Indian nations might one day form alliances with Spain or England and threaten national security. Removal would lessen that risk.

Though many lawmakers greeted the bill enthusiastically, others were appalled. New Jersey senator Theodore Frelinghuysen angrily declared, "We have crowded the tribes upon a few miserable acres of our Southern frontier; it is all that is left to them of their once boundless forests; and still . . . our . . . [unsatisfied greed] cries, give! give! give!"[33]

After weeks of tumultuous debate, however, Congress narrowly approved the bill by a vote of 103 to 97. When Jackson signed it on May 28, 1830, he established a federal policy toward Native Americans that would dominate the nineteenth century. And though Jackson told Congress that removal would be voluntary, he was prepared to use force if necessary.

"The reaction of the American people to removal was predictable," writes noted Jackson biographer Robert V. Remini. "Some were outraged. Others seemed uncomfortable with it but agreed that it had to be done. Probably a large number of Americans favored removal and applauded the President's action in settling the Indian problem once and for all. In short, there was no overwhelming public outcry against it."[34]

Jackson now had nearly unrestricted options. "The President," writes Peter Nabokov, "had both the power to select the tribes that were to be removed and the

---

A French Observer Describes the Forced Removal of the Choctaw

Alexis de Tocqueville, the French traveler who made many astute observations about the developing American society, recorded his personal impressions of the misery of the Choctaw removal in his classic book, Democracy in America.

At the end of the year 1831 I was on the left bank of the Mississippi, at the place the Europeans called Memphis. While I was there a numerous band of Choctaws . . . arrived; these savages were leaving their country and seeking to pass over to the right bank of the Mississippi, where they hoped to find an asylum promised to them by the American government. It was then the depths of winter, and that year the cold was exceptionally severe; the snow was hard on the ground, and huge masses of ice drifted on the river. The Indians brought their families with them; there were among them the wounded, the sick, newborn babies, and the old men on the point of death. They had neither tents nor wagons, but only some provisions and weapons. I saw them embark to cross the great river, and the sight will never fade from my memory. Neither sob nor complaint rose from that silent assembly. Their afflictions were of long standing, and they felt them to be irremediable. All the Indians had already got into the boat that was to carry them across; their dogs were still on the bank, [and] as soon as the animals finally realized that they were being left behind forever, they all together raised a terrible howl and plunged into the icy waters of the Mississippi to swim after their masters.

This portrait of a Choctaw chief was painted in 1834, just a few years after thirteen thousand Choctaw were driven from their Mississippi home.

squelched open debate, and finally persuaded some tribesmen to sign in favor of removal."[35]

The Choctaw Are Removed First

The Choctaw of Mississippi were the first to feel the heavy hand of the federal government. Although most of the twenty thousand Choctaw opposed removal plans, in 1830 some of their tribal representatives succumbed to government bribes and signed the Treaty of Dancing Rabbit Creek, which required the Indians to abandon their homes and give up 10.5 million acres (42,500 sq. km) to the U.S. government.

In late 1831 thirteen thousand Choctaw men, women, and children began a four hundred-mile (644-km) journey, traveling in ox-drawn wagons, on horseback, and on foot. Armed soldiers accompanied them to make sure they did not falter or run away. The trek became a death march. Winter temperatures plummeted below zero as pneumonia killed Choctaw by the hundreds. When warm, rainy weather returned, cholera felled hundreds more. The situation grew worse when government contractors and federal agents responsible for the Indians' welfare cheated them out of food and supplies. Altogether, two thousand Indians died.

Back in Mississippi, the remaining Choctaw, who were scheduled to follow in a second migration, balked when news

money—half a million dollars [authorized by Congress]—to finance the giant exodus." To ensure at least the appearance of voluntary migration, however, Jackson employed underhanded, if not illegal, methods. Nabokov continues, "Jackson's secret agents bribed, deceived, and intimidated individual Indians, falsified records, of the death march reached them. Instead of departing, many clung to their homelands, as whites swarmed onto their lands. "Our tribe has been woefully imposed upon of late," wrote one Choctaw to a white friend in 1850:

> We have had our habitations torn down and burned; our fences destroyed, cattle turned into our fields & we ourselves have been scourged, manacled, fettered and otherwise personally abused until by such treatment some of our best men have died. These are the acts of those persons who profess to be the agents of the Government to procure our removal to the Arkansas and who cheat us out of all they can by the use of fraud, duplicity, and even violence.[36]

The army had much less trouble with the Chickasaw. Overrun by settlers in Mississippi, many of these Native Americans had already migrated west several years before. Those left behind signed away their lands and also headed west, facing many difficulties along the way.

The Cherokee Go to Court

Georgia's Cherokee resisted. Instead of waging war, however, they fought legal battles—something they had done successfully in the past. In 1802 the federal government had threatened to extinguish Indian land titles in Georgia, but backed down when courts affirmed a 1785 treaty between the Cherokee and the United States that guaranteed Cherokee lands and declared them off-limits to non-Indians. Two similar treaties in 1791 and 1797 had reaffirmed the boundary lines of Cherokee land.

In 1827 the Cherokee antagonized whites by proclaiming themselves an independent nation in northwest Georgia. Angry Georgia lawmakers declared the Cherokee nation null and void in 1832, and extended state laws over the Cherokee that required the Indians to serve in the U.S. military and pay taxes, even though the Cherokee people were denied civil rights such as the ability to testify in court, vote, or hold public meetings. Georgia law even forbade Cherokee to mine gold on their own lands.

The Cherokee took their case to the U.S. Supreme Court, seeking an injunction to stop Georgia from stripping the tribe of its sovereign powers. However, in October 1832 the Court refused to consider *Cherokee Nation vs. Georgia*, ruling that Indians were domestic dependent nations, or wards of the United States, not independent foreign nations with sovereignty rights. This meant they could not turn to the courts for help. This decision also authorized Georgia to take actions that would destroy Cherokee forms of government.

Dying on the Trail of Tears

The Cherokee suffered another legal setback in 1836. In New Echota, Georgia, tribal strife erupted when Cherokee learned that a small group of their own men had met with white officials and signed a treaty calling for removal of all Cherokee. One of the signers, an Indian chief known as Major Ridge, acknowledged, "With this treaty, I sign my death warrant."[37] He was right. Unknown assassins killed Ridge and two others. Angry Cherokee also repudiated

The Cherokee Plead for Justice

Infuriated by the actions of Georgia legislators, Andrew Jackson, and the federal government, the Cherokee made a public appeal for justice in a declaration known as the Memorial and Protest of June 22, 1836. This excerpt is quoted in The National Experience: A History of the United States, *edited by John M. Blum.*

[At first, with U.S. government guidance,] the Cherokees were happy and prosperous and . . . they made rapid advances in civilization, morals, and in the arts and sciences. Little did they anticipate, that when taught to think and feel as the American citizen, and to have with him a common interest, they were to be despoiled by their guardian, to become strangers and wanderers in the land of their fathers, forced to return to the savage life, and to seek a new home in the wilds of the far west, and that without their consent. An instrument purporting to be a treaty with the Cherokee people, has recently been made public by the President of the United States, that will have such an operation, if carried into effect. This instrument, . . . [we] aver before the civilized world, and in the presence of Almighty God, is fraudulent, false upon its face, made by unauthorized individuals, without the sanction, and against the wishes, of the great body of the Cherokee people.

the treaty, claiming the men had no authority to act in behalf of all Cherokee, and vowed never to leave their lands.

In response, Jackson's successor, Martin Van Buren, ordered the U.S. Army to forcibly eject the Cherokee from their Georgia homelands. In May 1838 state and federal troops flooded into northern Georgia, surrounded seventeen thousand Cherokee, and forced them into guarded camps. Days later the soldiers forced the shocked Indians to begin a long and treacherous one thousand-mile (1,600-km) exodus along what is now called "the Trail of Tears." Their destination was the unorganized region west of the Mississippi River called Indian Territory, covering most of present-day Oklahoma, Kansas, southern Nebraska, and eastern Colorado.

On October 1, 1838, 645 wagons rolled westward, filled with weeping and heartbroken Cherokee and their hastily grabbed possessions. Georgians seized abandoned Cherokee lands even before the Indians had vacated the area. Wasted by disease, exposure, and starvation, nearly four thousand Cherokee—nearly one-fourth of all tribal members—died en route.

U.S. Troops Oust the Creek

Twenty-four years earlier, the Creek of Alabama, defeated in war by the U.S. Army, had ceded 23 million acres (93,000 sq. km) to the U.S. government. In 1832 the

Creek sadly watched as white squatters overran their remaining lands. That same year, tribal leaders signed a treaty requiring them to yield an additional 5 million acres (20,200 sq. km). Meanwhile, a different parcel of 2 million acres (8,000 sq. km) was redistributed to individual Creek rather than to the tribe as a whole. Though some Indians accepted these allotments, others refused and migrated to the southern portion of Indian Territory.

Those who had accepted allotments soon lost them. Within days white settlers seized the Indian properties, unimpeded by the federal government. Instead, federal agents imposed another treaty on the Creek to accept total removal. After a band of outraged Creek attacked encroaching whites,

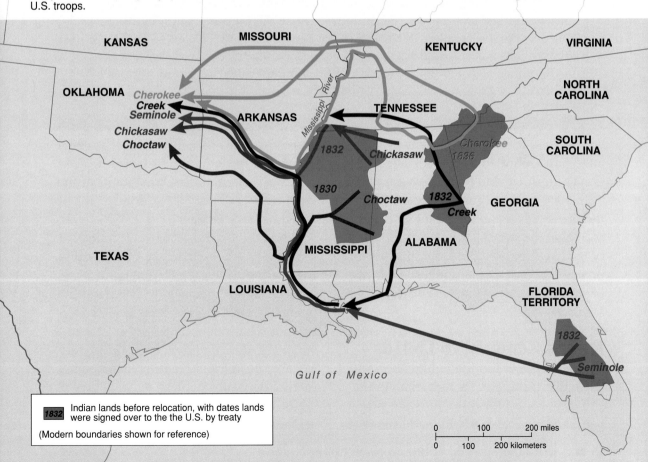

Removal of the Five Civilized Tribes

The Cherokee, Chickasaw, Creek, Choctaw, and Seminole tribes were known as the Five Civilized Tribes because they maintained permanent homes, organized governments, and farmed the land. In 1830, U.S. president Andrew Jackson initiated the Indian Removal Act to relocate all Indians west of the Mississippi River, where they would receive new land guaranteed to be theirs forever. Many Indians resisted giving up their lands; an estimated 30,000 Indians died as a result of forced relocations to Indian Territory by U.S. troops.

ILLINOIS INDIANA OHIO PENNSYLVANIA

KANSAS MISSOURI KENTUCKY VIRGINIA

OKLAHOMA

Cherokee
Creek
Seminole
Chickasaw
Choctaw

ARKANSAS

NORTH CAROLINA

TENNESSEE

Mississippi River

1832

Chickasaw

Cherokee 1836

SOUTH CAROLINA

1830

Choctaw

1832

Creek

GEORGIA

TEXAS

MISSISSIPPI

ALABAMA

LOUISIANA

FLORIDA TERRITORY

1832

Seminole

Gulf of Mexico

1832   Indian lands before relocation, with dates lands were signed over to the the U.S. by treaty

(Modern boundaries shown for reference)

0   100   200 miles
0   100   200 kilometers

An Army Officer Laments Removing the Cherokee

The following excerpt of a letter written by Captain L.B. Webster to his wife on June 9, 1838, as quoted in The Cherokee People *by Thomas E. Mails, reveals Webster's conflicting emotions about forcibly removing the Cherokee from their homelands.*

We are said to be in the thickest settled portion of the Cherokee country, and the least civilized. There are about six thousand in our neighborhood—their houses are quite thick about us, and they all remain quietly at home at work on their little farms, as though no evil was intended them. They sell us very cheap anything they have to spare, and look upon the regular troops as their friends. . . . These are the innocent and simple people, into whose houses we are to obtrude ourselves, and take off by force. They have no idea of fighting, but submit quietly to be tied and lead away. If there is anything that goes against my conscience it is this work, and I would not do it, whatever might be the consequences, did I not know that there are thousands that would, and probably with much less feeling towards the poor creatures. . . . Orders are out to begin operations on the 12th. . . . I expect to see many affecting scenes before the business is over. Those that were in Georgia have already been collected, and sent to the principal depots, from whence they are sending to the West as fast as possible.

army troops swept into the area and hunted down all Creek—hostile and peaceful alike—and rounded them up for deportation to the other side of the Mississippi.

In 1836 military guards ejected fifteen thousand Creek and forced them to make their own westward journey of death. Half of the Creek either died along the way or perished from sickness, hunger, and heartbreak during the first years after their arrival in Indian Territory.

Forced Removal in Florida

The Seminole of Florida would soon suffer similar treatment. Though relative newcomers to the Florida peninsula, many Seminole nonetheless held land titles that dated back to the era of Spanish land grants. Moreover, the 1819 treaty by which Spain had ceded Florida to the United States provided that all inhabitants of the territory were entitled to all the rights of any other U.S. citizens.

When the United States took control of Florida, however, many whites scorned the Native Americans' rights and pressured them to yield land. To hasten the opening up of Florida lands, the new government had negotiated with seventy Seminole chiefs and signed the 1823 Treaty of Camp Moultrie. According to this agreement Seminoles would vacate coastal lands, as well as most of western Florida, and resettle in the central part of the state.

In the process, the Seminole lost 30 million acres (121,400 sq. km) of land. In return, the Indians were to receive farm tools, livestock, annual cash payments for twenty years, and food.

These concessions did not satisfy white settlers for long, however. "The present location [of the Indians] is in the pathway of our settlers," complained the Florida Legislative Council in 1829, "and has seriously impeded the settlement of the fairest part of Florida."[38]

The federal government responded in 1832 with a new treaty requiring the Seminole to vacate the central Florida lands granted them by the Treaty of Camp Moultrie, by 1835. Rather than submit, some Seminole chose to fight. Under the leadership of a fierce warrior named Osceola, they launched raids and attacks that led to full-scale war in 1835.

U.S. forces battled Indian guerrilla tactics for the next seven years. Osceola was captured and died in prison in 1838, but his followers fought on until they were nearly exterminated. In 1842 some four thousand surrendered and were removed to Indian Territory. The fighting ended as a few defiant bands of Seminole evaded federal troops and faded into the vast Everglades swamp of southern Florida. Although the Seminole tribe never officially surrendered, their departure from their traditional lands removed the last human obstacle to white settlement in Florida.

Defining the New Indian Lands

From the time the government began deporting southern Indian tribes to the

Under the leadership of Osceola, the Seminole carried out a series of raids and attacks on white settlers in Florida that eventually led to full-scale war.

region in 1831, the new Indian Territory was defined by what it was not: Indian lands now included all of the United States west of the Mississippi "and not within the States of Missouri and Louisiana or the Territory of Arkansas."[39] In effect it comprised any lands that were not yet official states or organized territories, and there was no federal government there. As more lands became states, the borders of Indian Territory steadily shrank.

By law the Indian lands were to be off-limits to most whites. Yet, almost immediately, writes Dee Brown, "a new wave of white settlers swept westward and formed the territories of Wisconsin and Iowa. This made it necessary for the policy makers in Washington to shift the 'permanent Indian frontier' from the Mississippi River to the 95th Meridian."[40] To keep the newly relocated Indians confined west of this new dividing line and to stop whites from encroaching into Indian Territory, the federal government established a string of military posts to police the border.

Armed Resistance in Illinois

As southern tribes struggled in vain to keep their lands, displaced Native Americans to the north sometimes tried to reclaim theirs. In 1832 bands of Sac and Fox, led by Chief Black Hawk, traveled east across the Mississippi and returned to lands they once held in the Illinois and Wisconsin Territories. Black Hawk had demonstrated his defiance in a speech to fellow warriors:

> From the day when the paleface landed upon our shores, they have been robbing us of our inheritance, and slowly, but surely, driving us back, back, back toward the setting sun, burning our villages, destroying our growing crops, ravishing our wives and daughters, beating our papooses with cruel sticks, and brutally murdering our people upon the most flimsy pretenses and trivial causes.[41]

Desperate for food, the Indians crossed back into familiar lands searching for game. But their arrival terrified white settlers in the Illinois Territory and prompted the governor to call on President Jackson for military assistance. Help arrived in the combined form of state militia and U.S. Army troops that finally drove the starving Indians back to the other side of the Mississippi. After this episode, often called the Black Hawk War, Jackson responded to demands of settlers and ordered the relocation of all other tribes still living in the Northwest Territory to the Indian Territory.

By 1842 Jackson's goal of forced relocation of all Native American tribes to west of the Mississippi had been achieved. Some thirty thousand Indians had died in the process; the survivors left behind ancestral lands and a way of life. Few would adjust successfully to the profoundly different conditions of their new homes.

Chapter Five

Losing Ground West of the Mississippi

The relocated southern tribes arrived in Indian Territory and discovered blistering hot summers and freezing winters. Flooding was all too common, as the Choctaw learned in June 1833, when one of the worst floods of the Arkansas River in history wiped out families, destroyed possessions, and ruined corn crops. Flies multiplied in the filthy waters. Diseases swept through the tribes. "Not a family but more or less sick; the Choctaws dying to an alarming extent," observed Francis W. Armstrong, acting superintendent of Indian Affairs for the Western Territory who was also a government agent for the Choctaw. "Near the agency there are 3,000 Indians and within the hearing of a gun from this spot 100 have died within five weeks."[42]

Newly arrived Indians had difficulties with other Native Americans already dwelling in Indian Territory. The Chickasaw, for example, could not establish settlements for over four years because the federal government failed to make the area safe from raids by "wild" Indians, such as the Delaware, Shawnee, Kickapoo, and other more numerous and bellicose peoples.

Many among the Five Civilized Tribes had trouble adapting to their new circumstances for other reasons. Writes historian Grant Foreman:

> The Chickasaws led a restless, unsettled life on the lands of the Choctaw Indians with no incentive nor opportunity to establish their government, schools, and other institutions, nor land upon which they could build their homes. To aggravate the demoralization resulting from their forced migration, the emigrants on the way through Arkansas contracted smallpox from which between 500 and 600 of their tribe died before the disease was checked by vaccination.[43]

In general, few provisions had been made by the federal government to help

A Kickapoo chief prays to the Great Spirit in this painting. The Kickapoo were one of many tribes that resented the incursion of displaced southern tribes in their territory.

Indian migrants resettle and adjust to their new environment. Such aid as there was usually came from Catholic, Baptist, and Methodist missionary groups who founded schools and churches to convert displaced Indians to Christianity and teach basic literacy and manual skills. Although Congress appropriated funds to provide Indians with supplies such as guns, plows, seed, kettles, traps, and blankets, many of these goods were long delayed or disappeared in transit because corrupt government officials, military leaders, and even tribal chiefs confiscated them for their own personal profit. Government food allotments were also dangerously scant. Daily rations often consisted of only meat, bread, and salt.

Despite these tribulations, dislocated Indians tried their best to farm, hunt nearby buffalo, and build new communities. And though their lives were bleak, many believed they were also safe from the white man. They were wrong. A tide of whites was headed their way.

Immigrants Push Westward

The public craving for land had many causes. In 1837 the nation reeled from a widespread economic crisis and thousands of factory workers in the North lost their jobs. At the same time, many poor farmers in the South went bankrupt and sold their small farms. Thousands of unemployed Americans joined the constant stream of emigrants who sought new lands

A Cherokee Testimony of Hard Times in Indian Territory

Rebecca Neugin, a Cherokee who as a child survived the Trail of Tears, described the hardships she and her people faced upon reaching Indian Territory to Grant Foreman, author of The Five Civilized Tribes *and a leading authority on removal.*

Very few of the Indians had been able to bring any of their household effects or kitchen utensils with them and the old people who knew how, made what they called dirt pots and dirt bowls. To make them they took clay and formed it in the shape desired and turned these bowls over the fire and smoked them and when they were done they would hold water and were very useful. We could cook in them and used them to hold food. In the same way they made dishes to eat out of and then they made wooden spoons and for a number of years after we arrived we had to use these crude utensils. . . . We had no shoes and those that wore anything wore moccasins made out of deer hide and the men wore leggins made of deer hide. Many of them went bare headed but when it was cold they made things out of coon skins and other kinds of hides to cover their heads.

and opportunities in the West, including lands along the Pacific called Oregon. To this point only a smattering of whites—fur trappers, miners, and explorers—lived in the region. However, the area's population grew after 1833 when glowing descriptions of the Oregon Territory appeared in the eastern press. Land-hungry Americans traveled west along the Oregon Trail, a wagon road that ranged 2,000 miles (3,220 km) from Independence, Missouri, across the Rockies, to the Willamette Valley in Oregon. By 1846 five thousand settlers had made the trip. Coming fast behind them were thousands of Mormons, members of the Church of Jesus Christ of Latter-Day Saints, fleeing persecution in the east, who would end their trek in Utah Territory and carve out a thriving religious community.

At first most of these pioneers disregarded the Great Plains of the Midwest—a region nicknamed the "Great American Desert" because it was arid, almost void

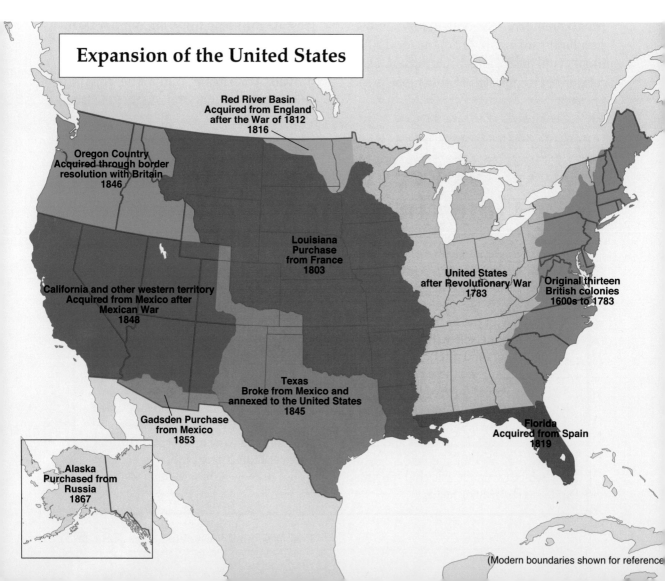

Expansion of the United States

Red River Basin
Acquired from England
after the War of 1812
1816

Oregon Country
Acquired through border
resolution with Britain
1846

Louisiana
Purchase
from France
1803

United States
after Revolutionary War
1783

Original thirteen
British colonies
1600s to 1783

California and other western territory
Acquired from Mexico after
Mexican War
1848

Texas
Broke from Mexico and
annexed to the United States
1845

Gadsden Purchase
from Mexico
1853

Florida
Acquired from Spain
1819

Alaska
Purchased from
Russia
1867

(Modern boundaries shown for reference

of trees, and hard to plow. Instead of homesteading here, settlers tried to cross the vast plains as quickly as possible. In time, though, others would realize these lands contained some of the most fertile soil in the world. In the 1830s and 1840s, though, the destination was the far West. To reach America's extreme western regions, many pioneers proceeded directly through Indian Territory. Alarmed Native Americans kept vigil on an ever-growing number of wagons, horses, oxen, and dogs trespassing their lands. Moreover, pioneer families were not the only whites to enter without permission.

Texas to the Pacific

"Scarcely were the refugees settled behind the security of the 'permanent Indian frontier' when white soldiers began marching westward through the Indian country," notes Dee Brown. "The white men of the United States . . . were marching to war with the white men who had conquered the Indians of Mexico."[44]

Americans had been migrating to Texas, a former province of Mexico, since the early 1820s. What began as a trickle of immigrants, though, became a torrent after the United States defeated Mexico in a war over boundary disputes in 1848. The United States ended up with two-fifths of Mexico, a vast area that stretched from Texas to California now opened up to American settlers. The United States added even more land in 1853, when Mexico sold to the federal government a strip of territory that today makes up the southern stretches of Arizona and New Mexico.

With that addition the United States owned contiguous territory from the Atlantic to the Pacific. For Native Americans, this development was menacing: The Indian Territory, already under considerable stress, was now an island in a sea of territory belonging to the land-hungry United States.

Gold Seekers Rush into California

Another stampede of settlers to the West began when gold was discovered in northern California in 1848. Miners, prospectors, and opportunists of all sorts from around the world rushed to the area, hoping to strike it rich. To get there many rode through Indian Territory, killing buffalo, trampling pastureland, and shooting Indians.

More than a few decided to stay on Indian lands, once again dismissing the inhabitants as inferior savages unfit to be stewards of the lands they possessed. In 1850 an editor for a Kansas newspaper wrote what many westerners believed: Indians were "a set of miserable, dirty, lousy, blanketed, thieving, lying, sneaking, murdering, graceless, faithless, gut-eating skunks as the Lord ever permitted to infect the earth, and whose immediate extermination all men, except Indian agents and traders, should pray for."[45]

Trying to Keep the Peace at Fort Laramie

As tensions between the Indians and the whites grew, the federal government sponsored a major conference of both groups in September 1851 at Fort Laramie, a military outpost in Wyoming charged with

Geronimo Recalls the Arrival of Whites in the Southwest

The famous Apache leader Geronimo recalls his impressions of the "coming of white men" into Apache lands in his autobiography Geronimo: His Own Story.

[Around 1858] we heard that some white men were measuring land to the south of us. In company with a number of other warriors I went to visit them. We could not understand them very well, for we had no interpreter, but we made a treaty with them by shaking hands and promising to be brothers. Then we made our camp near their camp, and they came to trade with us. We gave them buckskin, blankets, and ponies in exchange for shirts and provisions. We also brought them game, for which they gave us some money. We did not know the value of the money, but we kept it and later learned from the Navajo Indians that it was very valuable.

Every day they measured land with curious instruments and put down marks which we could not understand. They were good men, and we were sorry when they had gone on into the west. They were not soldiers. These were the first white men I ever saw.

Apache chief Geronimo resisted white settlers that encroached upon Apache land.

About ten years later some more white men came. These were all warriors. . . . At first they were friendly and we did not dislike them, but they were not as good as those who came first.

After about a year some trouble arose between them and the Indians, and I took the warpath as a warrior, not as a chief. I had not been wronged, but some of my people had been, and I fought with my tribe; for the soldiers and not the Indians were at fault.

providing security on the Oregon Trail. An estimated ten thousand men, women, and children from many various tribes and bands—Cheyenne, Arapaho, Sioux, Crow, and others—arrived on horseback and on foot dressed in full colorful tribal regalia to negotiate a treaty with the United States. The conference was the largest single meeting of Native Americans in history.

It also appeared to result in a successful treaty. Tribal representatives worked out acceptable boundaries among themselves and also promised white agents they would not molest pioneers on the Oregon Trail. They also acknowledged the United States had a right to maintain the trail and erect army forts to protect it.

In return the United States agreed to pay the Indians $50,000 a year for the next fifty years in the form of food, supplies, domesticated animals, and tools. Later, however, the U.S. Senate reduced to ten the number of years during which these payments, called annuities, would be made.

The U.S. government signed a similar treaty with Comanche and Kiowa tribes at Fort Atkinson on the Arkansas River in present-day Kansas. The Indians were to

In 1851 Indians from several tribes gather outside Fort Laramie, Wyoming, where a treaty was signed that protected pioneers along the Oregon Trail from Indian attack.

receive goods for ten years; in exchange, the United States could build and protect roads for immigrants, notably the Santa Fe Trail, an eight hundred-mile (1,290-km) road that led from Independence, Missouri, to Santa Fe, New Mexico.

These agreements, however, did little to keep the peace on the Plains; the massive numbers of whites settling on Indian lands overwhelmed all good intentions. "The permanent Indian country was dying fast," writes author Ralph K. Andrist:

> Already the frontier that was to have divided it forever from the white man's world had bulged and given way along a great section under pressure from land-hungry settlers. The myths about the worthlessness of grasslands [the Great Plains] were evaporating; pioneers had learned that tall-grass prairies land, at least, was tremendously fertile. The Indians had been pushed off almost all the prairie land of Minnesota and Iowa—part of the original permanent Indian Country—by the weary method of land cession treaties, and bigger things were ahead.[46]

By the early 1850s new groups were lobbying to open up more western territory to development. Some were businessmen who planned to build a railroad from the East to the Pacific coast. As the government managed to secure agreements with the Plains tribes, it also imposed treaties on Indians in the far western regions to give up 157 million acres (607,000 sq. km) of land encompassing Idaho, Oregon, and Washington.

An Old Controversy in New Territories

As whites moved west, they took with them a bitter debate that was tearing up the nation: the issue of slavery. A new wrinkle of the controversy soon emerged: Should slavery be allowed in the new western territories?

In an attempt to retain a balance of slave versus nonslave states, Illinois senator Stephen A. Douglas, chairman of the Committee on the Territories, pushed an act through Congress in 1854 that created two new territories, partly out of Indian Territory land: Nebraska in the north, Kansas in the south. The settlers of each new territory would determine whether slavery would be allowed when the territory achieved statehood. It was expected that Kansas would permit slavery and Nebraska would not.

To clear the way for settlement in Nebraska, the government made treaties with the region's Omaha, Ottoe, Missouria, Sac and Fox, Iowa, Kickapoo, Delaware, Shawnee, Kaskaskia, Peoria, Wea, Piankashaw, and Miami inhabitants. Sad and angry, but believing that at long last their homelands would be permanently fixed, Indians made concessions, giving up 13 million acres (52,600 sq. km) and retaining about one-tenth as much land for themselves. Some tribes exchanged their land for cash. Others received nothing.

"Too Worthless Ever to Be Wanted"

The 1854 territorial reorganization left the Five Civilized Tribes in southern Indian Territory, now shrunk to roughly the area

This Currier & Ives lithograph depicts a train full of whites steaming west along a track that stretches beyond the horizon. Two Indians on horseback in the right foreground take in the scene.

of present-day Oklahoma. Most U.S. observers agreed that this land was, as Andrist writes, "too worthless ever to be wanted by white men, and that the Indians living there could possess it indefinitely without being molested."[47]

Whites, however, did want this land. They even encroached onto cramped Indian reservations, violating all treaties and ignoring Indian protests. "Already the white population is occupying the lands between and adjacent to the Indian reservations," wrote George W. Manypenny,

commissioner of Indian affairs in his annual report of 1854, "and even going west of and beyond them, and at no distant day, all the country immediately to the west of the reserves, which is worth occupying, will have been taken up."[48]

So far, immigrants came mostly from the East. But in his report, Manypenny also observed the arrival of disappointed gold prospectors and others from the West, who came "sweeping like an avalanche from the Pacific coast, almost overwhelming the indigenous Indians in [their] approaches."[49]

Manypenny witnessed undisguised land theft in 1854 when white speculators and settlers began building the city of Leavenworth on Delaware lands. U.S. Army officials—charged with protecting Indians from such encroachment—merely stood by. "Trespasses and depredations of every conceivable kind have been committed on the Indians," wrote Manypenny in 1856. "They have been personally maltreated, their property stolen, their timber destroyed, their possessions encroached upon, and divers other wrongs and injuries done them."[50] Despite urgent protests from Manypenny and others, the federal government did nothing to stop the activities of the land-grabbing settlers.

At the time many Americans saw no real reason for anyone to help Native Americans because they believed God was allowing the country's original inhabitants to disappear from Earth. Horace Greeley, editor of the *New York Tribune*, visited the reservations of the Delaware and Potawatomi in 1859 and expressed this viewpoint: "These people must die out—there is no help for them. God has given this earth to those who will subdue and cultivate it, and it is vain to struggle against His righteous decree."[51]

The Civil War Rebalances the Equation

Native Americans, however, had no intention of abandoning the struggle, and in 1861 something happened to give them hope: the outbreak of the American Civil War, which temporarily slowed the influx of whites to the West and diverted attention from fighting Indians. Like Americans everywhere, white westerners took up arms on the Confederate or Union side and fought each other wherever they could. Blue-coated Union troops even abandoned army forts in the West to pursue Confederate sympathizers, leaving settlers more unprotected against Indian attacks than ever before.

Tribal leaders across the West seized the opportunity. Now was the time, they urged their people, to exploit this division between whites and drive them out of Native American lands forever.

Chapter Six

The Indian Wars of the American West

When the Civil War diverted Americans' attention from western expansion in 1861, the Sioux in Minnesota, which had become a state in 1858, were among the first to revolt. Decades of encroaching settlers, broken treaties, and swindling traders had reduced these Plains Indians to living in misery, hunger, and smoldering resentment on a reservation 10 miles (16 km) long and 150 miles (240 km) wide, a tiny fraction of the vast territory they once roamed. Food and supplies from the federal government were slow to arrive at the Indian agency on the Yellow Medicine River, forcing the Sioux to beg for credit from white traders to avoid starvation. While some whites sympathized with the Indians, others were cruelly indifferent. "So far as I am concerned, if they are hungry let them eat grass,"[52] Indian trader Andrew Myrick remarked.

Tempers finally snapped on August 17, 1862, when four hungry Sioux braves returning from an unsuccessful hunt argued and goaded one another into killing four white settlers. News of the senseless slaughter terrified homesteaders across the prairies. Many Sioux also panicked, fearing white retaliation, and hurriedly whisked their families to safety away from the region. Others, though, wanted war. An estimated thirteen hundred warriors massacred whites young and old in the Minnesota River Valley. Among those killed was the trader Myrick, found with a wad of prairie grass stuffed into his mouth.

The Minnesota state government dispatched an army of volunteers to quell the Indian uprising. The Sioux, however, killed over four hundred whites before the volunteers overwhelmed them. White retribution was harsh. In 1863 Congress punished the Sioux by taking all their Minnesota lands and forcing them into Dakota Territory. There many settlers made no attempt to distinguish openly

In 1862 Sioux Indians rise up against settlers in Minnesota. Congress punished the Sioux by relocating the tribe to Dakota Territory.

hostile Indians from non-warlike tribes, shooting down any Native Americans they encountered.

A Crackdown in the Southwest

Whites in the Southwest, meanwhile, cracked down on the Apache, including the feared Mescalero band, which survived in the merciless heat of the Southwest deserts by raiding and stealing from other Indians, American settlers, and Mexicans. Their raids ended when New Mexico–based general James Carleton commanded Union troops—who were unable to find any Southern rebels to fight—to round up Mescalero instead. "The men are to be slain whenever and wherever they can be found," Carleton proclaimed. "The women and children may be taken as prisoners, but, of course, they are not to be killed."[53] Fearing annihilation, the Mescalero sur-

rendered and relocated to a 40-square-mile (104-sq.-km) reservation on a barren wasteland along the Pecos River in central New Mexico called Bosque Redondo (Spanish for Round Grove).

Next Carleton set out to remove all Indians in the Rio Grande Valley to open the region to American homesteaders. Among them were the pueblo-dwelling Navajo, whom Carleton ordered to relocate to Bosque Redondo by July 20, 1862. He warned that his troops would hunt down and drive out resisters.

The deadline arrived, however, and not one Navajo appeared for deportation. Infuriated, Carleton hired famed Indian fighter Kit Carson to lead an expedition to track down the defiant Indians. Over the next six months Carson's men killed Navajo, burned homes, and destroyed fruit trees, crops, and livestock. Finally in midwinter, freezing Navajo surrendered after being trapped in a steep, rocky canyon.

When spring 1863 arrived Carson's men forced over fifty-four hundred men, women, and children to undertake a 300-mile (483-km) "Long Walk" to Bosque Redondo and military outpost Fort Sumner. Hundreds died along the way. Soldiers shot those who could not keep up. "The Navahos had the fortitude to bear freezing weather, hunger, dysentery, jeers of the soldiers, and the hard three-hundred-mile journey," writes Dee Brown, "but they could not bear the homesickness, the loss of their land."[54] Yet, those trials were not their worst.

Life at Bosque Redondo

By all accounts Bosque Redondo was an awful place. Conditions were primitive, drinking water unsafe. The soil was not fit for farming. Moreover, Navajo were crowded together with their ancient enemy, the Mescalero. Lacking adequate shelter, many Indians burrowed like animals into the sand to avoid dying of exposure.

Heartbroken, sick, and starving, the nearly nine thousand Native Americans interned there had no choice but to rely on their white captors to stay alive. But because the fort lacked food, clothing, medicine, and other supplies, Indians died by the thousands. When desperate Navajo slipped away from the reservation without permission, Carleton's troops shot to kill.

After alarmed officials at the reservation notified Congress of the squalid conditions

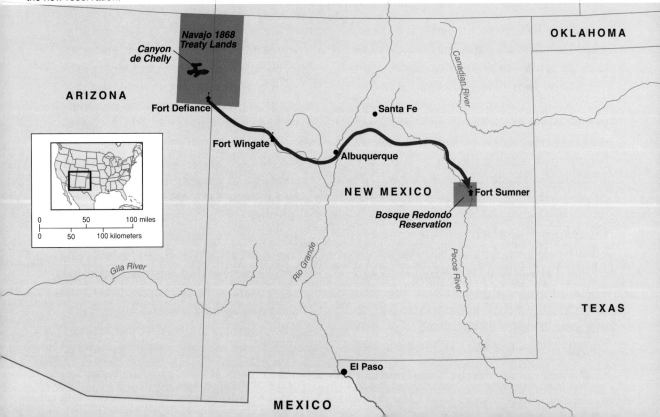

The Long Walk to Bosque Redondo

When the Navajo resisted U.S. general James Carleton's 1862 order to relocate to Bosque Redondo, Carleton ordered them hunted down and killed. Navajo survivors eventually surrendered after they were cornered in the narrow Canyon de Chelly. In March 1863, over 5,400 Navajo men, women, and children were forced to walk 300 miles to the 40-square-mile reservation called Bosque Redondo. Hundreds of Navajo died along the way, and many more died after arrival due to the infertile soil and harsh conditions on the new reservation.

In this 1865 photo, armed Union soldiers stand guard while Navajo use adobe bricks to build housing at the Bosque Redondo reservation in New Mexico.

at Bosque Redondo, the federal government launched an investigation. Officials later declared Carleton's relocation effort a disaster, reprimanded him, and reassigned him. Then in an uncommon move in the history of the West, the federal government released some seven thousand Navajo and allowed them to return to another reservation near their beloved native lands.

Clashes Escalate

Conflict also erupted in Colorado. There whites had swarmed onto Cheyenne and Arapaho lands, in violation of the 1851 Fort Laramie treaty, ever since gold was discovered near Pikes Peak in 1858. Indians at first tried to live in peace with the newcomers; but relations worsened as whites began to dominate the region.

In 1861 the U.S. government, disregarding Indian territorial rights, officially created the Colorado Territory, and negotiated a treaty with Cheyenne and Arapaho tribal leaders requiring them to cede their lands to the government and accept a small reservation in southeastern Colorado, located between the Arkansas River and Sand Creek.

From its onset the treaty generated bitter controversy. Whites expected the Indians to stay within the boundaries of the reservation at all times, but the Cheyenne believed the treaty only restricted where they established their homes. Since the reservation consisted mostly of uncultivatable land and lacked sufficient game, Indian hunters wandered beyond the reservation boundaries to hunt.

Eventually these hunting parties clashed with whites. Most of the fighting was episodic; but when the Arapaho butchered a family of four in Denver in May 1864 the territorial governor, John Evans, authorized a former preacher-turned-politician, John Chivington, to lead a militia against the Indians.

The volunteers first raided Cheyenne camps in northern Colorado. Then on May 16 they attacked a Cheyenne buffalo-hunting party in Kansas. Among those slain was Chief Lean Bear, a tribal leader who proudly wore a medal given him by President Abraham Lincoln during the chief's visit to Washington a year earlier.

News of these attacks provoked the Dog Soldiers—the elite Cheyenne warrior class —to seek revenge against all whites in both Kansas and Colorado. Writer Irving Stone summarizes the results: "The Indians made swift attacks on stages, mail coaches, freight trains, paralyzing passenger and food supply lines, earning Colorado the reputation as the most dangerous area in the United States to settle."[55]

The Sand Creek Massacre

Alarmed by the uprising, Evans called on all Colorado citizens "to be good patriots and kill all hostile Indians."[56] He also urged all friendly tribes to report to Fort Lyon in southwestern Colorado, where they would be fed and protected.

Although bloody fighting continued, two Indian leaders—Chief Black Kettle of the Cheyenne and White Antelope of the Arapaho—met with Evans, Chivington, and other whites in Denver to seek peaceful solutions. Indian leaders left the meeting, satisfied the talks had gone well and that peace would soon come.

A Condemnation of Colonel Chivington

A scathing passage from the report of an 1865 congressional committee on the massacre of Cheyenne Indians by Colonel John M. Chivington's troops appears in Wexler's Western Expansion.

As to the Colonel Chivington, your committee can hardly find fitting terms to describe his conduct. Wearing the uniform of the United Sates, which should be the emblem of justice and humanity; holding the important position of commander of a military district, and therefore having the honor of the government to that extent in his keeping, he deliberately planned and executed a foul and dastardly massacre which would have disgraced the veriest savage among those who were the victims of his cruelty.

White officials, however, viewed things differently. Evans, in fact, was distressed. He had recently formed a new regiment that was itching to see combat. "What shall I do with the third regiment if I make peace?" he asked one of his officers. "[They were] raised to kill Indians and they must kill Indians."[57] Meanwhile, bands of Arapaho and Cheyenne, seeking to comply with Evan's instructions, arrived at Fort Lyon on November 9, 1864. Base commander Major Scott J. Anthony ordered the Indians to camp along the banks of nearby Sand Creek and promised them military protection.

Chivington, however, had no intention of honoring Anthony's promise. Unable to find a band of Cheyenne to fight, he and the Third Colorado Volunteers launched a surprise attack against the sleeping Indians at Sand Creek at dawn on November 29. Chivington exhorted his men to "Kill and scalp all, big and little; nits make lice."[58]

Thus encouraged, the volunteers slaughtered Indian men, women, children, and even infants. Chivington's men also mutilated their victims and lifted bloody scalps as grisly souvenirs. By late morning, some two hundred Indians lay dead. During the onslaught White Antelope stood calmly beside his tipi, his arms raised in a gesture of peace. Chivington's men shot him to death. Black Kettle hoisted both an American and a white flag of surrender, but the soldiers kept firing. Against all odds, he survived the attack.

Later the volunteer soldiers rode into Denver, where residents hailed them as heroes. At a local theater Chivington exhibited one hundred scalps and regaled audiences with tales of the slaughter. Nationwide, however, news of the carnage evoked widespread condemnation. A military commission investigated the attacks, condemned Chivington, and relieved him of his command, but brought no criminal charges against him.

The massacre at Sand Creek galvanized Native American resistance, serving in particular to unite all tribes in Colorado. Stone describes the winter of 1864–1865 in Colorado as "an unrelenting reign of terror, the Indians destroying everything they could lay their hands on: telegraph lines, ranches, warehouses, devastating every mile of stage route . . . , attacking and killing soldiers at isolated forts."[59]

Trouble to the North

Within a year the Cheyenne and Arapaho uprising subsided. As Colorado quieted, however, trouble flared in the northwestern lands of the Sioux in Montana and Wyoming when whites appeared, feverishly searching for gold. To accommodate the prospectors, the federal government planned to build a road and a series of forts along the Powder River to give travelers from the East a protected route to the mining towns of Bozeman, Montana, and Virginia City, Nevada.

These plans were stymied by a band of Teton Sioux led by Chief Red Cloud, who refused to grant permission for this "Bozeman Trail" to be blazed through Indian lands. When the government pursued the project anyway, Red Cloud and three thousand warriors rampaged during the summer of 1866, killing both soldiers and civilians.

Colonel Chivington leads the charge against the Cheyenne at Sand Creek in 1864. Chivington's men slaughtered Indians of all ages, including children.

Striving for a Peaceful Solution to "the Indian Problem"

The Civil War had ended in 1865 and the American public wanted an end to the bloodshed in the West as well. In Washington political leaders clashed over what to do next. Westerners and conservatives demanded a harsh military crackdown on the warring tribes. Some called for even sterner measures, including the extermination of Indians.

In the end, more moderate voices, mostly those of easterners, prevailed by successfully urging Congress to adopt a policy of "humane" treatment of Indians. In 1867 the lawmakers instructed the so-called Peace Commission to negotiate with

western tribal leaders to "remove the causes of war; secure the frontier settlements and railroad construction; and establish a system for civilizing the tribes."[60]

Another goal was to remove Indians to small, localized reservations instead of large, centralized ones. Peace commissioners also offered Indians protection, food, and supplies if they submitted to U.S. authority and relocated to one of two major reservation regions. To their fellow Americans they suggested this: "To maintain peace with the Indian, let the frontier settler treat him with humanity, and railroad directors see to it that he is not shot down by employees in wanton cruelty."[61]

Critics, meanwhile, scoffed at the new government effort. "The peace policy was little more than a name," complained Episcopal bishop H.B. Whipple of Minnesota. "No change was made in the Indian system; no rights of property were given; no laws were passed to protect Indians."[62]

During the fall of 1867 leaders of the Cheyenne, Arapaho, Kiowa, and Comanche parlayed with federal peace commissioners at Medicine Lodge Creek in southern Kansas. Whites wanted the removal of all the tribes from their homelands to make way for the construction of a railroad along the Smoky River in Kansas. Indians, though, sought peaceful coexistence and the right to remain on their lands. Finally the Indians reluctantly agreed to cede their lands along the Arkansas and Canadian rivers in Indian Territory. They also promised to abandon their nomadic ways and relocate on a reservation between the Red and Washita rivers in western Indian Territory.

At Fort Laramie in 1868, peace commissioners also drew up a treaty with the rebellious Sioux; the government promised to abandon blazing the Bozeman Trail if the Sioux of Wyoming and Montana agreed to stop their raids and relocate to the Black Hills of the Dakotas. Here, on sacred lands, they would receive food and supplies from the government and instruction in farming and Christianity. Federal negotiators also promised to keep whites off Indian property, which was defined as all lands west of the Missouri River and east of the Rockies. This region was promised for the absolute and undisturbed use of the Sioux. Such a promise, again, proved impossible to keep.

In that same year Ute in Colorado succumbed to pressure and signed a treaty with the federal government. Their spokesman, Ourag, observed, "The agreement that an Indian makes to a United States treaty is like the agreement a buffalo makes with his hunters when pierced with arrows. All he can do is lie down and give in."[63]

Non-Treaty Bands Resist

Many Indians, however, refused to cooperate with the Peace Commission. The

In 1867 Indian leaders meet with government officials at Medicine Lodge Creek, Kansas. The Medicine Creek treaty ceded additional Indian land to whites.

Reaching the American Heart

In the preface to Helen Hunt Jackson's A Century of Dishonor, *dated November 11, 1880, H.B. Whipple, Episcopal bishop of Minnesota, recalls a moment of frustration in his effort to stave off the mass execution of rebellious Sioux in Minnesota.*

In 1862, I visited Washington, to lay before the Administration the causes which had desolated our fair state with the blood of those slain by Indian massacre. After . . . I pleaded in vain and received no satisfaction, Secretary Stanton said to a friend, "What does the Bishop want? If he came here to tell us that our Indian system is a sink of iniquity, tell him we all know it. Tell him the United States never cures a wrong until the people demand it; and when the heart of the people are reached the Indian will be saved."

"non-treaty bands" of Sioux, Arapaho, and Cheyenne, for instance, feared an end to their nomadic way of life and continued attacking whites across the plains from Texas to Kansas.

The federal government responded in 1867 by appointing a tough new commander of troops in the West—General William Tecumseh Sherman, who as a Union general had helped smash the South during the Civil War. Sherman's strategy was far different from that of the Peace Commission. "The more [Indians] we can kill this year," he said, "the less will have to be killed the next war . . . they all have to be killed or be maintained as a species of paupers."[64] Another officer who shared this view was one of the most zealous Indian fighters under Sherman's command, Lieutenant-Colonel George Armstrong Custer, whom the Indians called "Yellow Hair."

In the autumn of 1868, Black Kettle and other survivors of the Sand Creek mas-

sacre were trying to live peacefully with other Cheyenne in western Indian Territory on the upper Washita River. Fearful of being harmed during this army crackdown on hostile Indians, they approached General William B. Hazen, then commander of army forces in Indian Territory, and obtained a promise of protection. Yellow Hair, however, had other plans. A former rival of Hazen's, Custer disregarded his fellow officer's promise and ordered his 7th Cavalry regiment to attack the Cheyenne on the dawn of November 7, 1868. Here, on the banks of the Washita River, American troops repeated the carnage of Sand Creek, killing Black Kettle, his wife, and 101 other Indians.

The fate of those who failed to yield to the will of the United States seemed clear. However, pockets of defiant Indians in the West were not cowed by Yellow Hair or the might of the U.S. government. Their struggle was not yet over.

Chapter Seven

Native American Last Stands

More blood flowed after Custer's attack on the Washita River. In fact, U.S. Army troops battled Indians in the West over two hundred times between 1869 and 1877. These military campaigns followed decades of raids with civilian participation: Between 1848 and 1870, for example, vigilante groups helped kill between fifty thousand and seventy thousand Indians in northern California and forced the survivors into reservations. With the death of each Native American, whites came closer to achieving total domination of North America's native peoples. A coalition of Indian warriors, however, temporarily slowed this process with a stunning victory that sent shock waves through the United States.

In the summer of 1874 Custer, still in command of the 7th Cavalry, led more than twelve hundred men on an expedition into the Black Hills of western Dakota—the sacred lands of the Sioux forbidden to whites by treaty. Officially Custer and his men were simply exploring an uncharted region, but soon they located what they really had hoped to find: gold. News of their discovery spread fast. "There is gold in the hills and rivers of the region," read an editorial in the Chicago *Inter Ocean*, "and the white man desires to take possession of it. . . . [The Indians] must decrease that the new comers may grow in wealth. Happy for him the day when the last of the tribes shall fold his blankets around his shrunken limbs, and take his final sleep, to waken in the eyes of the Great Spirit."[65]

The 1868 Fort Laramie Treaty had promised the Sioux that no person lacking tribal permission "shall ever be permitted to pass over, settle upon, or reside in the territory."[66] These words left little room for reinterpretation. But when miners, settlers, and commercial agents swarmed into the area, the government did little to oust them. Instead it offered to buy the Indian lands. The Sioux scorned the offers; their warriors, along with Cheyenne forces, gathered in Montana and prepared for war.

Defeat and Revenge

In December 1875 federal officials realized the growing danger and ordered all Indians to vacate their settlements in the Black Hills of the Dakota and Wyoming territories and move to reservations or face military reprisals. The Indians remained defiant. In the spring of 1876 the army dispatched three regiments, each approaching from a different direction, with instructions to converge on the Indians.

On the morning of June 25, 1876, the six hundred exhausted men of Custer's regiment neared an Indian encampment along

General George Armstrong Custer held all Indians in absolute contempt and believed it was the duty of whites to kill off as many Indians as possible.

Indian warriors outflank Custer's doomed regiment during the battle at Little Big Horn in 1876. Custer and most of his men were killed during the skirmish.

the Little Big Horn River, deep in Sioux Territory. Custer ignored orders to wait for reinforcements before attacking, divided his men into three groups, and recklessly sent them to charge what he thought was a minor Sioux camp.

Custer famously blundered. What his men rushed into was a major stronghold of up to ten thousand Indians, including over twenty-five hundred Sioux, Cheyenne, Arapaho, and Crow warriors, led by Chiefs Sitting Bull, Crazy Horse, and Rain-in-the-Face. The Indians quickly surrounded and closed in on Custer's doomed force.

In less than a half-hour, Custer and some 225 soldiers—about one-third of his regiment—lay dead. Across the West, Indians cheered the news of Yellow Hair's death. Their euphoria, however, was short-lived.

Smashing Indian Power on the Northern Plains

The timing of the clash known as Custer's Last Stand proved disastrous for Indians, occurring unfortunately just as the nation was celebrating its one hundredth birthday. In a burst of patriotic anger, many outraged Americans demanded the federal government avenge Custer's death and solve once and for all what was seen as the "Indian problem."

Volunteers from across the nation signed up to fight Indians. Newspapers demanded retribution. "Killing a mess of Indians is the only recreation our frontier rangers want,"[67] a *Dallas Daily Herald* editorial cried.

A few white leaders, though, blamed Custer for the disaster. This number included President Ulysses S. Grant, commander of Union forces during the Civil War. Grant shared his expert opinion with the *New York Herald:* "I regard Custer's massacre as a sacrifice of troops, brought on by Custer himself, that was wholly unnecessary."[68]

Nonetheless, the federal government mobilized army troops to punish Plains Indians. Within months blue-coated soldiers had defeated the northern Cheyenne in Montana's Powder River country and the Sioux in South Dakota along Cedar Creek. In the spring of 1877 three thousand more Cheyenne and Sioux, including Crazy Horse, the greatest warrior of the northern Plains, surrendered after his warriors succumbed to the relentless pounding of American artillery.

The once-defiant Plains Indians, who had roamed the continent for centuries, now faced a bleak and heartbreaking removal to reservations in Indian Territory near the Missouri River. Indian power on the northern Great Plains was broken.

War Against Indians Is Inevitable

Appearing in Evan S. Connell's Son of the Morning Star, *this excerpt from an article in the* Bismarck Tribune *on June 17, 1874, predicts the Indian war that will be launched by Custer's expedition into the Black Hills.*

This is God's country. He peopled it with red men, and planted it with wild grasses, and permitted the white man to gain a foothold; and as the wild grasses disappear when the white clover gains a footing, so the Indian disappears before the advances of the white man.

Humanitarians may weep for poor Lo [Indians], and tell the wrongs he has suffered, but he is passing away. Their prayers, their entreaties, can not change the law of nature; can not arrest the causes which are carrying them on to their ultimate destiny—extinction.

The American people need the country the Indians now occupy; many of our people are out of employment; the masses need some new excitement. The war is over, and the era of railroad building has been brought to a termination by the greed of capitalists and the folly of [farmers' opposition]; and depression prevails on every hand. An Indian war would do no harm, for it must come, sooner or later.

A Failed Escape in Montana

Though the Sioux War of 1876–1877 marked the last major Indian war, one final episode of Indian resistance occurred in 1877, carried out by the Nez Percé (Pierced Noses), under one of Native Americans' greatest leaders, Im-mut-too-yah-lat-lat, known in English as Chief Joseph.

During the 1850s whites first appeared on Nez Percé lands in Idaho and Oregon. Yielding to the inevitable white demands for their land, the Nez Percé ceded a section of their territory and relocated to government reservations. White desire for even more land prompted a federal order compelling the Nez Percé to move again in 1877, this time to the Lapwai Reservation in Idaho. Forgoing armed resistance, Joseph persuaded his people to do as the government demanded. While the move was under way, however, several warriors launched a series of deadly retaliatory raids against white settlers.

Fearing military reprisals, Chief Joseph led his people—150 warriors and 550 other men, women, and children—on a wild and daring 1,400-mile escape through Montana and Wyoming toward safe haven in Canada. Exhausted, tattered, and starving, the Nez Percé faltered just forty miles shy of the Canadian border and were intercepted by army troops. After a five-day battle, the Indians reluctantly agreed to the terms offered by Colonel Nelson Miles: "If you will come out and give up your arms, I will spare your lives and send you to your reservation."[69]

Although some Nez Percé warriors managed to escape soon afterward, most of the tribe surrendered, expecting to be returned to Idaho as Miles promised. But they were grievously mistaken. Over Miles's objections, his army superiors ordered the Nez Percé to live in Indian Territory. Here Joseph's six children and a full one-fourth of his tribe died broken and sick.

In 1877 Chief Joseph of the Nez Percé tribe led his people in one final episode of resistance against the whites.

Chief Joseph Calls for Dignity

Chief Joseph was a leader of the Nez Percé, a Pacific Northwest tribe that made a heroic attempt to reach Canada rather than submit to living on a reservation. U.S. Army troops, however, captured the Nez Percé as they neared the Canadian border in 1877 and forced them onto the Lapwai Reservation in Idaho. In this following passage, taken from Native Americans: Opposing Viewpoints, *edited by William Dudley, Chief Joseph makes a poignant plea for justice as he witnesses the suffering and death of his people on the reservation.*

I only ask of the Government to be treated as all other men are treated. If I can not go to my own home, let me have a home in some country where my people will not die so fast. . . . When I think of our condition my heart is heavy. I see men of my race treated as outlaws and driven from country to country or shot down like animals.

I know that my race must change. We can not hold our own with the white men as we are. We only ask an even chance to live as other men live. We ask to be recognized as men. We ask that the same law shall work alike on all men. If the Indian breaks the law, punish him by the law. If the white man breaks the law, punish him also.

Let me be a free man—free to travel, free to stop, free to work, free to trade where I choose, free to choose my own teachers, free to follow the religion of my fathers, free to think and talk and act for myself—and I will obey every law, or submit to the penalty.

In 1885 the government, believing that Chief Joseph and 150 others might again stir up the Nez Percé, shipped them to the Coville Reservation in Washington, where they remained isolated from their families and communities for the rest of their lives. There, on September 1, 1904, the reservation's doctor wrote that Chief Joseph died of a "broken heart."[70]

After the surrender of the Nez Percé, all that remained were isolated pockets of Indian resistance. Kiowa and Comanche rebellions on the southern Plains were crushed in 1878, as was a Ute uprising in Colorado. The same fate awaited the Klamath in southern Oregon. In 1881 Sitting Bull and his band surrendered at Fort Buford, North Dakota. In the Southwest, after years of marauding and raiding whites in New Mexico and Arizona, the fabled warrior chief Geronimo and his band of Apache became prisoners of the Americans in 1886.

By this time the West had changed dramatically. Railroads and telegraph wires stretched across former wilderness, cutting across the trails of the near-extinct buffalo and former Indian lands. Towns had sprung up along railroad tracks. Mine shafts marked the sites of organized industrial operations. Barbed-wire fences enclosed thousands of ranches and pastures. And everywhere in the great American West, Indians were overpowered, decimated, and corralled onto cramped, barren reservations.

The Dreamer Religion and the Ghost Dance

From the gloom, despair, disease, and poverty of the shattered and displaced Indians arose a spiritual awakening called the Dreamer Religion. An intensely spiritual blend of Indian and Christian beliefs, the new religion urged Indians to reject white culture and dominance.

An important part of the Dreamer Religion was the Ghost Dance, a ritual devised by a Paiute visionary named Wovoka, who claimed that during a solar eclipse he received a message for Indians from the Great Spirit: "They were to give up European—now American—ways," writes author Annette Rosenstiel, "return to the old customs practiced before the Europeans arrived, and to the simple life, with no guns, no alcohol, and no trade goods. And, if the Indians performed the Ghost Dance, the religion's chief ritual, the whites would disappear, the land would be returned to the Indian people, and all the great warriors of former times would come back to earth."[71]

A Ghost Dance would last days at a time as Indians moved to the hypnotic pounding of drums. Some warriors wore "ghost shirts," which they believed would make them immune to the white man's bullets. On the reservations Native Americans of all ages danced relentlessly, waiting for a Christ-like savior to come.

One tribe after another adopted the haunting Ghost Dance with its feverish vision of a final struggle with the whites, a reunification with dead ancestors, and a restoration of the nearly vanished buffalo herds; meanwhile, nearby settlers, miners, and Indian agents feared an Indian uprising was imminent. In mid-November 1890 a terrified employee of the Pine Ridge Reservation telegraphed, "Indians are dancing in the snow and are wild and crazy. . . . We need protection and we need it now. The leaders should be arrested and confined at some military post until the matter is quieted, and this should be done at once."[72]

Fearing the worst, local authorities summoned the 7th Cavalry—Custer's former regiment. They also banned the Ghost Dance and ordered the arrest of Indian leaders suspected of stirring up a rebellion. But when the great Sioux leader Sitting Bull was killed resisting arrest on a reservation, grief-stricken Sioux mourners danced into an even greater frenzy.

In December 1890, as tensions mounted on the reservations, Sioux chief Big Foot led a band of three hundred men, women, and children to join other Sioux dancing in the South Dakota Badlands. On their way, soldiers of the Seventh Calvary confronted them and arrested Big Foot, one of the suspected "fomenters of disturbances."[73]

Tragedy at Wounded Knee

Big Foot's people did not resist. Instead they peacefully traveled with the soldiers toward a nearby fort. On December 28, 1890, the Indians, under guard, camped along a creek called Wounded Knee. The next morning, uneasy army troops circled the Indians with Hotchkiss guns, a type of small cannon, and ordered them to surrender their weapons.

The fearful Sioux refused to surrender their guns. Suddenly someone fired—historians disagree over who it was—and instantly the U.S. Army raked the Indians with blazing gunfire, killing 90 men and 200 women and children. Many bled to death in the snow. "We tried to run," recalled Louise Weasel Bear, "but they shot us like we were buffalo. I know there are some good white people, but the soldiers must be mean to shoot children and women. Indian soldiers would not do that to white children."[74]

Four days later the soldiers stacked the frozen corpses into a mass grave and posed for photographs. Twenty-six members of the company later were awarded Congressional Medals of Honor, but the incident has gone down in history as a shameful example of injustice toward Native Americans and the near annihilation of a people and culture.

Soldiers pile Sioux corpses into a mass grave at Wounded Knee. Ninety Indian men and two hundred women and children were gunned down in the 1890 massacre.

Reflecting on the White Dominance of Native Americans

While many Americans lamented the American conquest of Indian lands, others expressed no regret whatsoever. Wrote Theodore Roosevelt in *Winning of the West* in 1889:

> Unless we were willing that the whole continent west of the Alleghanies should remain an unpeopled waste, the hunting-ground of savages, war was inevitable; and even had we been willing, and had we refrained from encroaching on the Indians' lands, the war would have come nevertheless, for then the Indians themselves would have encroached on ours.[75]

Native Americans were angry, depressed, and grief-stricken. "Sometimes at evening I sit, looking out on the big Missouri [River]," Buffalo Bird Woman of the Hidatsa tribe recalled years later:

> The sun sets, and dusk steals over the water. In the shadows I seem again to see our Indian village, with smoke curling upward from the earth lodges; and in the river's road I hear the yells of the warriors, the laughter of little children as of old. It is but an old woman's dream. Again I see but shadows and hear only the roar of the river; and tears come into my eyes. Our Indian life, I know is gone forever.[76]

Thus, at long last, American military power had resolved the issue of land ownership. A pressing question, however, remained: What was to be done now with the two hundred thousand dispossessed Native Americans?

Chapter Eight

Losing Ground on the Reservations

By the close of the nineteenth century, nearly all Native Americans lived on one hundred federal Indian reservations, most of which were located in the West. They had no other choice. In 1871, in fact, General Philip Sheridan, the commander of the military operation on the Great Plains, forbade Indians to even leave the reservation without a pass from white authorities.

For the federal government, the reservation system made logistical sense. As a superintendent of the Bureau of Indian Affairs (BIA), the federal organization directly responsible for dealing with Indians, once remarked: "In history the U.S. government discovered that it was cheaper to keep them on the reservations than to try and kill them. So, they were marched into what we hoped were useless pieces of land."[77]

But the reservations meant disaster to Indians. Defeated in war, uprooted from their tribal lands, they were now completely at the mercy of whites for their protection and welfare.

No longer could Native Americans negotiate treaties with the federal government. They lost this right in 1871, when Congress formally ended the recognition of Native Americans as sovereign nations. Lawmakers did vow to honor treaties made before 1871. This promise, however, was hardly reassuring to most Indians, since the federal government had violated almost all of the four hundred treaties it had made in the previous century. From this moment onward, Indians were to be considered wards of the United States, subject to congressional laws, agreements, and presidential decrees, instead of negotiated treaties.

Stripped of their status as sovereign peoples, the Native Americans faced a long future of legal challenges by non-Indians. Worse still, Congress, freed from the constraints of treaties, often cut off or reduced the annuities it had promised to

A Comanche poses with his horse and dogs on a desolate reservation in this nineteenth-century photo. Reservations were typically situated on barren and undesirable land.

pay to Indians. Unscrupulous Indian agents also diverted to the black market many Indian supplies that should have gone to the people on the reservations. As a result, Native Americans faced increased malnutrition, disease, and other social ills.

Indian Reform or Ruin?

As the twentieth century approached, reformers and Indian haters alike agreed it was no longer possible for Indians to follow traditional practices and that Native Americans should be assimilated into American mainstream life and culture. And the best way to do this, according to U.S. policy makers, was to abolish what remained of traditional Indian ways, creating an indigenous population of English-speaking Christians who farmed for a living.

During the 1880s, federal officials, believing education to be the best way to facilitate assimilation for Indians, set up hundreds of day schools and many boarding schools to teach young Indians the basics for living in a white person's world in areas such as cooking, mechanics, and farming. To run these institutions, white preachers, teachers, and various volunteers descended on the reservations intent on erasing Indian languages, customs, and spiritual practices and replacing them with their own ways. These agents of change believed they were acting in the best interest of the Native Americans, but most showed extraordinary cultural insensitivity. Many Indian children were uprooted from their tribes and sent far away to live and learn at the white schools. Sometimes preachers or former military officers at the schools punished students who tried to escape or clung to their native ways. Some school authorities even punished Indian children for merely speaking their own languages.

"By the mid-1800s, the United States had banned most forms of Indian religion on the reservations," points out Indian historian Little Rock Reed. "Indians who maintained tribal customs were subject to imprisonment, forced labor, and even punishment by starvation. Indian dress, ceremony, dances, and singing were forbidden. Sacred instruments, medicine, and pipes were confiscated and destroyed. Even Indian names and hairstyles were forbidden by law."[78] Such efforts undermined Indian family unity and tribal authority, degraded Indian culture, and helped pitch Indians into depths of despair.

The Dawes Act

In 1887, Congress took another step toward solving the "Indian problem" by passing the Dawes Severalty—or General Allotment—Act, named for its sponsor, Senator Henry L. Dawes of Massachusetts. To implement the act, federal agents surveyed Indian land, evicted non-Indian settlers, and then reapportioned or "allotted" land in smaller sections back to the Indians on a severalty or individual basis rather than to the tribe as a whole. Each family, for example, was entitled to receive 160 acres (0.65 sq. km), while unmarried adults and orphans under age eighteen could obtain 80 acres (0.33 sq. km). Children who lived with their parents were allotted 40 acres (0.16 sq. km). Twice as much land could be allotted if the property was suitable only for grazing, and not farming. "By

Native American students attend class at a boarding school in Pennsylvania in this 1903 photo. Such schools were part of the government's plan to assimilate Indians into white society.

President Arthur Calls for "Civilizing" Indians

In 1881 U.S. president Chester A. Arthur addressed the nation's "Indian problem" in his annual address, with words that foreshadow the creation of the Dawes Act. The following is excerpted from Commager's Documents of American History.

We have to deal with the appalling fact that though thousands of lives have been sacrificed and hundreds of millions of dollars expended in the attempt to solve the Indian problem, it has until within the past few years seemed scarcely nearer a solution than it was half a century ago. . . .

[To make a success of the effort to] introduce among the Indians the customs and pursuits of civilized life and gradually to absorb them into the mass of our citizens, sharing their rights and holden to their responsibilities, there is [an important need for new laws]. . . .

My suggestions [are]: . . . The passage of an act making the laws of the various States and Territories applicable to the Indian reservations within their borders. . . . The Indian should receive the protection of the law . . . [and] be allowed to maintain in court his rights of person and property. . . .

Of greater importance is . . . the enactment of a general law permitting the allotment in severalty, to [those Indians who want it] . . . a reasonable quantity of land secured to them by patent, for their own protection made inalienable for twenty or twenty-five years . . . .

In return for such considerate action on the part of the Government, . . . the Indians in large numbers would be persuaded to sever their tribal relations and to engage at once in agricultural pursuits. Many of them realize . . . that their hunting days are over and that it is now for their best interest to conform their manner of life to the new order of things.

allotting reservation land in severalty," writes Janet A. McDonnell in *The Dispossession of the American Indian 1887–1934*, "policy makers hoped to replace tribal civilization with a white one, protect the Indians from unscrupulous whites, promote progress and save the federal government money."[79]

The Dawes Act was a boon to whites. Federal agents designated lands left over after all allotments had been made as "surplus" lands that could be sold to non-Indians to raise money for Indian supplies. Many Native Americans suspected that some government officials designated more desirable parcels of lands as surplus to benefit whites.

The Dawes Act originally stipulated that "allotted Indians"—that is, those who accepted allotment—were eligible for U.S.

citizenship. But this presented a problem, because as citizens Indians would have to pay property taxes, and if they were unable to do so, they stood to lose their lands to anyone who settled outstanding tax bills.

Troubled by this possibility, Congress amended the act, allowing the government to hold all allotted Indian lands in trust for twenty-five years. During this period, Indians were both exempt from paying taxes and prohibited from selling their lands. By forbidding early sales of the allotted lands, Congress hoped to prevent Indians from squandering their holdings and to protect them from being fleeced by underhanded land agents. When the trust period ended, the government would issue formal deeds allowing Indian landowners to do with their land as they pleased.

Liberal reformers and humanitarians had high hopes for the Dawes Act, believing it would help Indians assimilate successfully into mainstream American society. Many conservatives, land speculators, and individuals hoping to acquire land at bargain prices also favored the Dawes Act, but for entirely different reasons. They thought the initial reservation system set aside a disproportionate amount of public land to Indians, a "vanishing race." But under the allotment system, they reasoned, Indian lands held by individuals, rather than tribes, would be easier to transfer to whites.

The Failure of Allotment

Despite the good intentions of its supporters, the Dawes Act was a disaster for Indians. From the onset, tribal authority suffered a blow when the government parceled out land to individuals instead of

In 1887 Senator Henry L. Dawes sponsored an act that gave each Native American family its own parcel of land.

to entire tribes. In addition, the goal of turning Indians into self-sufficient farmers who would wean themselves off government assistance proved elusive. For one thing, some Indians became dependent on government rations and saw no need to farm. Moreover, many Indian males held to traditional attitudes that agriculture was "women's work" unsuitable for hunters and warriors.

Even those Indians who did take up farming encountered many problems that often doomed their best efforts. Not only did they generally lack experience in modern farming techniques, most did not have sufficient equipment, seed, and livestock to establish themselves. Worse yet, land allotments were often arid, barren, and lacked access to water.

Losing Ground on the Reservations ■ 81

Inheritance problems also complicated Indian attempts at farming. If an Indian died before his trust period ended, the Dawes Act specified that his heirs were to divide his property. Over generations, this subdivision resulted in land division into smaller and smaller units that were ultimately too small to farm economically. Many Indians sold such unusable, unconsolidated parcels to white speculators, who could afford to buy multiple small lots and reconstitute the original, more valuable, allotments.

Eventually Congress took action to prevent further splintering of Indian holdings by allowing Native Americans to sell inherited property before the trust period expired and split the profits among the heirs. Although this new rule was meant to help Indians, it actually sped up the process of Indian land sales to eager white buyers.

Another problem with the Dawes Act was that many Native Americans—for example, the very young and the very old—were incapable of farming. Thus in 1891 Congress again amended the act, to permit Indians who could not do agricultural work to seek government approval to lease their lands to non-Indians.

Apaches line up for beef at an Arizona reservation in this woodcut. By the end of the nineteenth century, many Indians found themselves dependent on such government rations.

In 1893 wagons and buggies roll past storefronts and rows of tents in the newly settled Oklahoma Territory.

Three years later lawmakers exempted additional Indians from the antileasing rule. Once again, these changes merely made it easier for land-hungry whites to obtain Indian lands. But allotment was not the only means used in the late nineteenth century to take land away from Native Americans. Other forces were also at work, particularly in Oklahoma.

The Oklahoma Land Rush

By the late 1880s what was left of Indian Territory was under siege. For years federal troops tried to keep land-hungry settlers out of the territory without much success. Finally Congress gave in to pressure and authorized that 2 million acres (8,100 sq. km) of the "Unassigned Lands," or Oklahoma District, in the western part of

the territory be opened to homesteading. On April 22, 1889, sixty thousand people rushed into the district to stake a claim. In 1890 the newly settled lands became the Oklahoma Territory. Other similar land runs took place over the next six years, as Indian Territory was increasingly diminished, until all that was left in Native American hands were lands directly held by the Five Civilized Tribes. Soon the federal government also carved up these lands under the Dawes Act. Surplus land once again ended in white possession.

As Indians and federal agents squabbled over the details of allotment, many impatient or unscrupulous whites contrived ways to take possession of remaining Indian lands. They squatted illegally on Indian lands, tricked Native Americans out of their properties, and even murdered landholders to get what they wanted. Unaware of the true value of real estate and confused by the concept of landownership, many Indians sold their holdings much too cheaply.

Meanwhile, one of the Indians' greatest fears was fast becoming a reality. Native Americans in Oklahoma had long opposed having their lands incorporated into a state or federal territory. Repeatedly, government officials had assured tribal leaders that such a thing would never take place. But in 1907 yet another official white promise vaporized when the Oklahoma Territory was joined with the fragmentary remains of the Indian Territory to become the forty-sixth state of the United States.

Even after Oklahoma joined the nation as a state, the pressure to get Indian land continued. Again whites argued that Indians were not suitable stewards for the few parcels of land they still had. Only whites, they said, knew what to do. "I hold

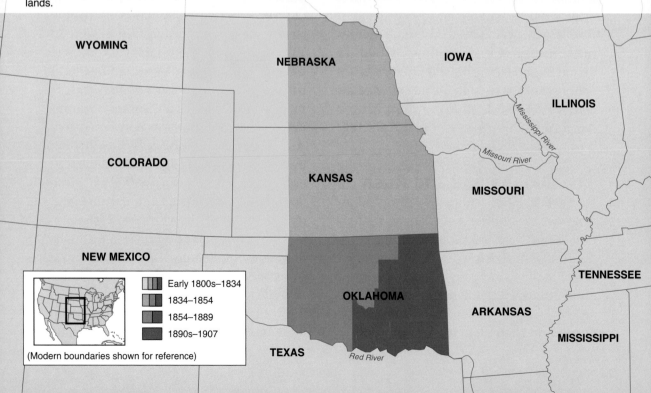

Indian Territory

By the early 1800s, the general area north of the Mexican border (now Texas) and west of the Mississippi was thought of as Indian Territory, and several northeastern tribes had already moved to the area. In 1830, President Andrew Jackson and Congress passed the Indian Removal Act, designating a "permanent Indian frontier" west of Missouri and Arkansas. Individual tribes were granted their own parcels of land within these boundaries; some tribes had very small parcels and others maintained much larger pieces of land.

In 1854, Kansas Territory was officially created and 18 million acres of northern Indian Territory were opened for white settlement. Throughout the late 1800s, various new bills and treaties further reduced the Indians' promised land, until 1907 when Congress joined Indian Territory with Oklahoma Territory to create the new state of Oklahoma. The Indians of Indian Territory no longer ruled their own lands.

NORTH DAKOTA
MINNESOTA
WISCONSIN
WYOMING
NEBRASKA
IOWA
ILLINOIS
COLORADO
KANSAS
MISSOURI
Mississippi River
Missouri River
NEW MEXICO
TENNESSEE
OKLAHOMA
ARKANSAS
MISSISSIPPI
TEXAS
Red River

Early 1800s–1834
1834–1854
1854–1889
1890s–1907

(Modern boundaries shown for reference)

it to be an economic and social crime in this age and under modern conditions," insisted Cato Sells, commissioner of the BIA, in 1913, "to permit thousands of acres of fertile land belonging to the Indians and capable of great industrial development to lie in unproductive idleness."[80]

Two years later the BIA enabled whites to obtain these lands more easily by changing the Dawes Act to exempt "competent" Indians from the twenty-five-year trust period. This change authorized twenty-one-year-old Indian landowners with at least a sixth-grade education and at least one Indian parent to dispose of their lands as they pleased. The result was an even greater selloff of Indian lands to whites.

Lone Wolf's Losing Battle

The U.S. government's attempt to obtain lands Indians did not wish to part with did not stop with the blatant manipulation of Oklahoma. For instance, the treaty that originally set up the Kiowa and Comanche reservations clearly required that three-fourths of all adult males had to approve any sale of Indian reservation land. Nevertheless, federal agents quietly worked out an agreement with fewer than the required numbers of Indian representatives who agreed to sell tribal land to whites

In 1903 a Kiowa named Lone Wolf challenged such a treaty violation in court. His lawsuit also argued that federal agents had falsely represented how much the federal government was willing to pay for any surplus land. Ultimately the case was heard by the Supreme Court, which ruled against Lone Wolf. In Lone Wolf's suit against Ethan Hitchcock, the Secretary of the Interior, the Court ruled that Congress had reserved the right to break treaties with Indians when it deemed such actions to be in the best interest of the government and Indians; moreover, the Court said it had no jurisdiction to interfere with such matters: "Plenary [absolute] authority over the tribal relations of the Indians has been exercised by Congress from the beginning, and the power has always been deemed a political one, not subject to be controlled by the judicial department of the government."[81] According to the court, the Indians possessed only occupancy rights, which could be "transferred" if the United States saw fit. In effect, Indians now had no legal recourse against federal control of tribal lands.

Chapter Nine

Holding On to What Is Left

Judicial rejection of tribal authority coincided with a population explosion in the United States, particularly in the West. Between 1890 and 1920 the U.S. population increased by 68 percent. Demand for, and the price of, the most desirable farmland in the East rose accordingly. Increasingly, settlers eyed for development the arid and semiarid western lands that whites had once been content to allot to Indians. "It was no longer enough for Indians to accept allotments and surrender the surplus land to whites; they were expected to use their own allotted land profitably or surrender it,"[82] writes historian Janet McDonnell.

And so during the 1920s and 1930s, Indians were encouraged, often pressured, to sell, lease, and cede their lands to whites at an alarming rate. From 1887 to 1934 Indian landholdings shrank from 138 million acres (558,500 sq. km) to 52 million acres (210,400 sq. km.). Two-thirds of all Native Americans were now either land-less or lacked enough acreage to live off the land. As a result they became even more dependent on the government, a situation that was the exact opposite of what reformers intended when they launched the Dawes Act.

Buffeted by Politics

The abuses facilitated by the Dawes Act ended with the presidency of Franklin D. Roosevelt, elected in 1932 at the height of the Great Depression. Roosevelt's New Deal programs to boost the economy and put millions back to work extended to Indian affairs. John Collier, a staunch defender of Indian rights who served as Roosevelt's commissioner of Indian affairs, helped to draft the Indian Reorganization Act of 1934, which halted allotment and banned the unregulated sales of Indian lands. Furthermore, it authorized the federal government to buy back "surplus" lands and restore them to tribal hands. The act also strengthened tribal authority by empowering Indians to govern themselves with elected representatives.

With Collier's help, many Indians formed their own tribal corporations to boost economic development on the reservations. The federal government also spent $70 million building new schools, clinics, roads, community centers, irrigation systems, and other community projects on Indian reservations. The Indian Reorganization Act also set up the Court of Indian Affairs, which removed Indian tribes from the authority of state judiciaries.

Collier's actions pleased many Indians but generated controversy. An array of conservative lawmakers in Congress claimed his policies were "un-American" because they kept Indians apart from mainstream American society. Collier resigned in 1945 amid criticism of all federal Indian programs. Some insisted that Native Americans had proved they could assimilate in the modern world without government help by serving with U.S. military forces in the recently ended World War II. Others simply argued that Indian

In 1934 Indian Commissioner John Collier, pictured here with Hopi chiefs at a ceremony in Washington, D.C., helped draft the Indian Reorganization Act, which banned the unregulated sale of Indian lands.

support programs were too expensive. In 1946, for example, one Oklahoma official complained that the country could expect to pay up to $2 billion for Indians during the next fifty years. "They do not need a Federal guardian now," he argued, "nor will they need one for the next 50 years!"[83]

Oklahoma congressman George B. Schwabe went even further and demanded the abolition of the BIA. "It is a drain upon the taxpayers," he insisted, "[and] a poor guardian for the Indians. I think it tends to encourage paternalism and socialist and . . . communistic thinking."[84]

At the time many Americans agreed. In the post–WWII era the United States faced a new rival—the Soviet Union, whose totalitarian rule, government-controlled economy, and international ambitions frightened many Americans. Anti-Communist hysteria would sweep the United States in the 1950s, prompting many to become suspicious of Native Americans and their communal way of life.

By the late 1940s many conservative Republicans in Congress demanded a new federal Indian policy based on termination, the ending of government control, supervision, and support of Native Americans. This policy included plans to dismantle Indian reservations, undo all treaties, cancel all federal responsibilities for Indian welfare, and end Indian tribal life. In this way advocates of termination hoped to reverse Collier's efforts to promote self-determination for Indian tribes and instead assimilate Indians into mainstream American life.

Attempting to "Terminate" America's Reservations

The termination idea proved controversial among both whites and Indians. Writes historian Donald Fixico:

Indian Appreciation of Franklin D. Roosevelt

That many American Indians appreciated the efforts of President Franklin D. Roosevelt to improve their lives is shown in this passage from a letter of tribute written to Senator Elmer Thomas of Oklahoma after the president's death in 1945, excerpted from Donald Fixico's Termination and Relocation: Federal Indian Policy in the 1950s.

I am taking the privilege of speaking for all my Indian people of our land, that in the passing of Franklin Delano Roosevelt, we have lost a great friend. The news of his death personally was a shock to me. I don't know what will become of our people in the future. We all know the long-range planning for the welfare of our people he had established. There will never be a greater man in an age to do justice for them.

Those who agreed with federal officials were primarily mixed-bloods, while those who believed that Indians were still considerably different from white Americans were full-bloods. Many mixed-bloods stated that they were tired of government restrictions on their properties and wanted them lifted. They professed that the federal trust status made Indians second-class citizens. The majority of this group of Indians was ready to join the mainstream society, but the full-blood faction objected.[85]

Many full-blooded Indians opposed termination because they feared it would bring cultural annihilation. They also suspected that once again white lawmakers were conniving to turn Indian lands over to white timber, ranching, mineral, and real estate interests.

As the termination movement gained strength, lawmakers introduced another controversial idea. It was time, they said, to let Indians seek monetary rewards for the losses they suffered at the hands of the federal government.

The Indian Claims Commission

In 1946 Congress established the Indian Claims Commission, an agency to which Native Americans could submit claims against the United States for lands improperly taken. Liberal supporters of this idea maintained that at long last Indians had a

In 1946 President Harry Truman signs a bill establishing the Indian Claims Commission, an agency that sought to protect Indian lands.

chance to receive at least cash payments for their great land losses.

Others denounced the plan. "Why must we buy America from the Indian all over again?"[86] demanded one Republican congressman. Despite opposition, however, during the next decade Native Americans collected over $500 million in settlements for loss of lands taken during the nineteenth century. Not all claims were approved: Over a thirty-year period, Native Americans won 101 cases, but lost 133.

A Blackfoot Leader Speaks Out Against Termination

Though a few Indian tribes agreed to terminate the U.S. government's trustee relationship, most did not. Many openly fought the policy. One outspoken opponent was Earl Old Person, who served as the chairman of the Blackfoot tribe of Montana. This selection is part of a speech Old Person gave in 1966, reprinted in Dudley, Native Americans.

In our Indian language the only translation for termination is to "wipe out" or "kill off." We have no Indian words for termination. And there should be no English word for termination as it is applied to modern day terms regarding the relationship of the U.S. Government and the American Indian. Why scare us to death every year by going to Congress for money and justifying the request on the grounds that the money is necessary to "terminate the trust relationship of the U.S. to the American Indian"?

You have caused us to jump every time we hear this word. We made treaties with the U.S. Government which guaranteed our right to develop our reservations and to develop as a people free from interference. In order to bring about this development, careful planning must be done on the part of not only the agencies of the Government, but by the tribes themselves. But how can we plan our future when the Indian Bureau constantly threatens to wipe us out as a race? It is like trying to cook a meal in your tipi when someone is standing outside trying to burn the tipi down.

So let's agree to forget the termination talk and instead talk of development of Indian people, their land, and their culture.

Blackfoot chief Earl Old Person staunchly opposed the policy of termination and called on the federal government to continue to accept responsibility for Indian welfare.

During the late 1940s protermination lawmakers pounced on the claims policy, arguing that because lawsuits were now enriching Indians, all other means of federal economic assistance should be cut off. Conservatives further argued that once the claims process had run its course, Congress would have met its final financial obligation to Native Americans and the U.S. government should bear no future responsibility for Indians. This course spelled disaster for Native Americans: By 1950 over half of all Indians still lived in poverty on reservations, and Native Americans were America's poorest ethnic group no matter where the remainder had relocated.

Some tribes, however, refused to apply for much-needed cash settlements, even though they did not have the option of reclaiming their lands. Said a spokesman of the Blackfoot tribe, "Our land is more valuable than your money. It will last forever. It will not even perish by the flames of fire. . . . We cannot sell the lives of men and animals; therefore we cannot sell this land. It was put here by the Great Spirit and we cannot sell it because it does not belong to us!"[87]

An Era of Termination

In 1953 Republican president Dwight D. Eisenhower officially implemented a termination policy. Under this plan all tribes had to dispose of their lands in one of two ways: Indians had to form a corporation to manage their lands under a trustee of their choosing, or they had to sell off their lands and distribute the proceeds among tribal members.

Congress also directed the BIA to commence a relocation program for Indians from reservations to urban areas, where they were expected to become self-sufficient city dwellers. To hasten the process the government announced that it would reject claims for past land losses by tribes that would not agree to termination.

From 1954 to 1962, 109 tribes, bands, and various Indian groups liquidated, or sold off, their holdings under the rules of termination. This action pleased many conservatives, but brought great distress to Indians, as they watched their reservations and tribal identities vanish. Former reservation Indians experienced cultural shock and racial discrimination in America's cities. Because so many lacked skills needed to hold jobs in an urban environment, few could rise from poverty. Their health and life expectancies ranked lowest in the nation, and their suicide rate was twice that of the general population.

By 1958 the Eisenhower administration realized termination was a huge mistake and stopped implementing the policy, unless Indians requested it. "The termination policy simply evaporated in the early 1960s because not enough advocates could be found in Congress to make it an important issue," writes Indian historian Vine Deloria Jr. "By 1958, Indians were beginning to go to the polls in increasingly larger numbers and would retaliate against senators and congressmen who suggested a break in the traditional federal-Indian relationship. Many persons in Congress might have wanted to sever the relationship, but it was a hazardous position to maintain at election time."[88]

Native American Lands in the United States

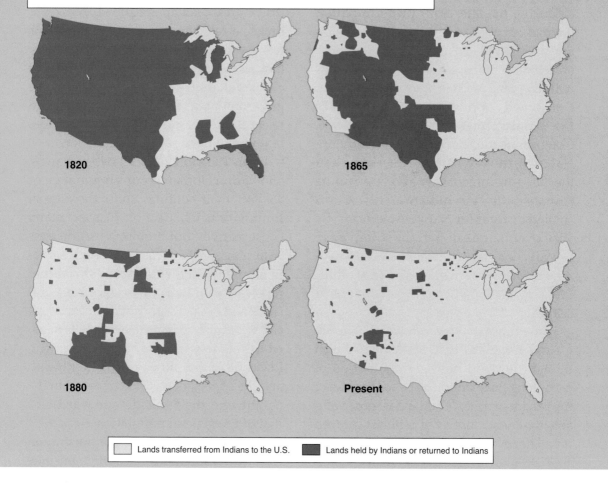

1820

1865

1880

Present

Lands transferred from Indians to the U.S.   Lands held by Indians or returned to Indians

Modern Indian Policy Changes

Attitudes toward Native Americans improved during the presidency of Texan Lyndon Baines Johnson from 1963 to 1968. Johnson, a Democrat, proposed government support that would lift Indian standards of living to levels of average mainstream Americans. An even more historic shift in policy for Indians came from the Republican administration of President Richard Nixon in the 1970s. Nixon urged Congress to repeal the termination law completely, and announced a policy that gave greater self-government to Native Americans, with the federal government helping to upgrade educational, legal, and medical services on reservations.

Many Indians were surprised and encouraged when the Nixon administration broke with tradition in 1970 and convinced Congress to return to the Taos Pueblo of New Mexico 48,000 acres (194 sq. km) of mountainous territory taken by the federal government in 1906, including Blue Lake, one of the tribe's most sacred sites. This action marked the first time Native Americans were compensated for lost territories with restored title to land, not cash payments.

Modern Legal Struggles

In the ensuing decades the federal government maintained the policy of greater tribal self-government introduced during the Nixon era. Indian activism peaked as more Native American tribes waged legal battles to recapture lands taken from their ancestors and sue for damages, with mixed results.

Some tribes won substantial settlements. In 1970, for example, the Supreme Court ruled that the Passamaquoddy and Penobscot of Maine had been unlawfully deprived of their lands in 1790 and were entitled to monetary compensation as well as the right to repurchase land. The tribes had originally sued the federal government for an astounding $25 billion and two-thirds of the territory of the state of Maine. After years of negotiation, a landmark settlement reached in 1980 awarded the tribes $81.5 million and purchase options to reacquire 300,000 acres (1,214 sq. km). This agreement also ended all future claims against the government by Indian tribes in Maine.

The Worst Is Over

Writing in American Indian Policy in the Twentieth Century, *contemporary Indian writer, scholar, and activist Vine Deloria Jr. argues that if conditions for Indians today are not improving, at least they are not getting worse.*

Human societies seem always to stumble upward toward a more sublime and humane ordering of their domestic relations. Despite our contemporary shortfalls, there is no question that we live in a better world, that we have more concern for the weak and helpless, and that we are evolving better and more comprehensive ways of handling our human problems.

Federal policy for American Indians shows the same line of progression as do other areas of policy consideration. A century ago Congress blithely and arrogantly dictated what would happen in Indian country and neither the Indians nor the federal agencies that served them had much to say about it. Today hardly a thought is voiced in the area of Indian policy without consultation with a wide variety of Indian people. Policy seems no worse today than it did in earlier eras of American history.

. . . Not only do we possess a keener sense of justice today, we also have a better sense of what is appropriate for communities.

. . . Today . . . reservations are encouraged to modify national programs to fit their particular needs, and no tribe is expected to carry out a program or policy in defiance of nature and good judgment.

In the 1980s the government sought to open up Arizona's San Francisco Peaks, land that is sacred to the Navajo and Hopi, to ski resort development and mining.

Other lawsuits were unsuccessful. For example, in 1978 the Wampanoag Indians of Mashpee, Massachusetts, lost a suit to win back 13,700 acres (55 sq. km) on Cape Cod. A jury concluded that the Wampanoag —one of the first tribes to greet the English over 350 years earlier—were no longer a tribe in 1870 when the disputed land was taken and therefore had no legal standing.

Some legal battles remain unresolved, notably those of the Lakota Sioux of South Dakota. In 1979 the Supreme Court ruled that the Lakota were entitled to monetary compensation, plus interest, for Black Hills

territory taken from them in 1877. A figure of $100 million was calculated at the time of the Supreme Court decision. The Lakota wanted their land back, however, not money, and the tribe refused the settlement. The designated settlement fund has since grown to over $500 million, but the tribe continues to refuse cash payment as it pursues the title to its former lands.

Altogether, Indians have increased their tribal holdings since the 1930s, when allotment practices finally ceased. Today, tribes own about 96 million acres (388,500 sq. km), or roughly 5 percent of all lands in the United States—a small fraction of the North American territory their ancestors once occupied.

Conflict over Land Use

The days of flagrant land theft, violence, massacres, forced relocation, and termination are gone. Nonetheless, government-sponsored pressure on Indian lands has occurred in recent decades. During the Reagan administration of the 1980s, for example, Interior Secretary James Watt sought to open up areas of the San Francisco Peaks in Arizona, lands sacred to the Navajo and Hopi, to ski resort development and mining leases.

Even relocation has recurred in modern times. In 1974 the federal government relocated thousands of Navajo who had long shared an Indian reservation in Black Mesa, Arizona, with Hopi Indians to make way for coal strip-mining operations. Many Navajo angrily objected. The consequences of this removal have been bad for both tribes, writes author Judith Nies: "Black Mesa has suffered human rights abuses and ecological devastation, the Hopi water supply has dried up; thousands of archeological sites have been destroyed, and, unbeknownst to most Americans, twelve thousand Navajos have been removed from their lands—the largest removal of Indians in the United States since the 1880s."[89]

More troubles came in 1988, when a federal court enabled the U.S. Forest Service to oust the Sioux from a section of the Black Hills—a clear violation, say Indian activists, of the Fort Laramie Treaty of 1868. A state park and public recreational areas were also established in Sioux territory in the Black Hills.

Today, the federal government retains vast power to take away Indian land. The United States, like other Western democracies, can cite the government's right of "eminent domain" as justification for confiscating land from nearly anyone for public use, such as for construction of a new airport or highway system. But unlike most other Western democracies, the United States has special land treaties with native peoples who live within the country's borders. These treaties offer no absolute protection to Native Americans, however. "There is nothing," writes scholar Sharon O'Brien, "to prevent Congress from taking treaty held lands."[90] Various court decisions since the nineteenth century have upheld the legislature's right to void existing land titles and Indian treaties; Congress, though, would have to compensate Native Americans for any loss of "treatied lands." Lands never officially recognized by treaty or law as belonging to their original inhabitants, however, may be confiscated without compensation.

These possibilities notwithstanding, the era of overt hostility between the U.S. government and Native Americans is over. Today more pressing concerns command the attention of tribal leaders, such as education, health care, poverty, and economic development. Many Native Americans also seek a way to engage the modern world, while retaining both their tribal lands and a way of life inherited from those who settled North America first.

Notes

Introduction: A Clash of Two Worlds

1. Quoted in Christopher Davis, *North American Indian*. London: Hamlyn, 1969, p. 67.

Chapter 1: A Lust for Land

2. Quoted in Daniel Boorstin, *The Discoverers*. New York: Random House, 1983, p. 248.
3. Quoted in Richard B. Morris and James Woodress, eds., *Voices from America's Past: Vol. 1, The Colonies and the New Nation*. New York: E.P. Dutton, 1961, p. 17.
4. Quoted in Alan Axelrod, *Chronicle of the Indian Wars: From Colonial Times to Wounded Knee*. New York: Prentice-Hall, 1993, p. 11.
5. Dee Brown, *Bury My Heart at Wounded Knee*. New York: Bantam, 1970, p. 3.
6. Gary Wills, *Under God: Religion and American Politics*. New York: Simon and Schuster, 1990, p. 140.
7. Quoted in George W. Manypenny, *Our Indian Wards*. New York: Da Capo, 1972, p. 13.
8. Quoted in Editors of the Reader's Digest Association, *Through Indian Eyes: The Untold Story of the American Peoples*. Pleasantville, NY: 1995, pp. 55–56.
9. Quoted in Mary Ellen Jones, ed., *Christopher Columbus and His Legacy: Opposing Viewpoints*. San Diego: Greenhaven, 1992, pp. 100, 102.
10. Quoted in Jones, *Christopher Columbus and His Legacy*, pp. 119–20.
11. Howard Zinn, *A People's History of the United States*. New York: Harper & Row, 1980, p. 16.

Chapter 2: Colonial Struggles for Control

12. Quoted in Axelrod, *Chronicle of the Indian Wars*, p. 73.
13. Quoted in Peter Nabokov, ed., *Native American Testimony: An Anthology of Indian and White Relations, First Encounter to Dispossession*. New York: Thomas Y. Crowell, 1978, p. 113.
14. Quoted in William Dudley, ed., *Native Americans: Opposing Viewpoints*. San Diego: Greenhaven, 1998, p. 59.
15. Quoted in Edward S. Barnard, ed., *Story of the Great American West*. Pleasantville, NY: Reader's Digest Association, 1977, p. 18.
16. Quoted in Manypenny, *Our Indian Wards*, p. 35.
17. Quoted in Sanford Wexler, *Westward Expansion: An Eyewitness History*. New York: Facts On File, 1991, p. 22.
18. Quoted in Henry Steele Commager, ed., *Documents of American History*. New York: Appleton-Century-Crofts, 1948, p. 49.
19. Quoted in Axelrod, *Chronicle of the Indian Wars*, pp. 101–102.

20. Quoted in Wexler, *Westward Expansion*, p. 23.

Chapter 3: U.S. Expansion: An Era of Broken Treaties

21. "Treaty with the Delawares: 1778," Avalon Project at Yale School. www.yale.edu/lawweb/avalon/ntreaty/del1778.htm.
22. Quoted in Commager, *Documents of American History*, p. 31.
23. Quoted in Davis, *North American Indian*, p. 45.
24. Quoted in Wexler, *Westward Expansion*, p. 59.
25. Quoted in Davis, *North American Indian*, p. 43.
26. Quoted in Rebecca Brooks Gruver, *An American History: Vol. 1, To 1877*. Reading, MA: Addison-Wesley, 1972, p. 195.
27. Quoted in Benjamin Capps, *The Indians*. New York: Time-Life, 1973, p. 153.
28. Quoted in Wexler, *Westward Expansion*, p. 76.
29. Quoted in Gruver, *An American History*, p. 205.
30. Quoted in John M. Blum et al., *The National Experience: A History of the United States*. 6th ed. San Diego: Harcourt Brace Jovanovich, 1985, p. 188.

Chapter 4: Forced Removal from The East

31. Quoted in Manypenny, *Our Indian Wards*, p. 99.
32. Quoted in Manypenny, *Our Indian Wards*, p. 101.
33. Quoted in Robert V. Remini, *The Life of Andrew Jackson*. New York: Harper & Row, 1988, p. 213.
34. Remini, *The Life of Andrew Jackson*, p. 215.
35. Nabokov, *Native American Testimony*, p. 187.
36. Quoted in Grant Foreman, *The Five Civilized Tribes*. Norman: University of Oklahoma Press, 1934, p. 75.
37. Quoted in Barnard, *Story of the Great American West*, p. 71.
38. Quoted in Wilfred T. Neill, *Florida's Seminole Indians*, St. Petersburg, FL: Great Outdoors, 1956, p. 16.
39. Quoted in Brown, *Bury My Heart at Wounded Knee*, p. 67.
40. Brown, *Bury My Heart at Wounded Knee*, p. 6.
41. Quoted in Dudley, *Native Americans*, p. 65.

Chapter 5: Losing Ground West of the Mississippi

42. Quoted in Foreman, *The Five Civilized Tribes*, p. 24.
43. Foreman, *The Five Civilized Tribes*, pp. 100–101.
44. Brown, *Bury My Heart at Wounded Knee*, p. 8.
45. Quoted in Davis, *North American Indian*, p. 57.
46. Ralph K. Andrist, *The Long Death: The Last Days of the Plains Indian*. New York: MacMillan, 1964, p. 21.
47. Andrist, *The Long Death*, p. 22.
48. Manypenny, *Our Indian Wards*, p. 122.
49. Manypenny, *Our Indian Wards*, p. 122.
50. Manypenny, *Our Indian Wards*, p. 126.
51. Quoted in Dudley, *Native Americans*, p. 134.

Chapter 6: The Indian Wars of the American West

52. Quoted in Wexler, *Westward Expansion*, p. 230.

53. Quoted in Brown, *Bury My Heart at Wounded Knee*, pp. 20–21.

54. Brown, *Bury My Heart at Wounded Knee*, p. 22.

55. Irving Stone, *Men to Match My Mountains*. New York: Doubleday, 1956, p. 335.

56. Quoted in Stone, *Men to Match My Mountains*, p. 336.

57. Quoted in Andrist, *The Long Death*, p. 87.

58. Quoted in Andrist, *The Long Death*, p. 87.

59. Stone, *Men to Match My Mountains*, p. 337.

60. Quoted in Barnard, *Story of the Great American West*, p. 226.

61. Quoted in Dudley, *Native Americans*, p. 123.

62. Quoted in Helen Hunt Jackson, *A Century of Dishonor (A Sketch of the United States Government's Dealings with Some of the Indian Tribes)*. Williamstown, MA: Corner House, 1973, p. viii.

63. Quoted in Nancy Wood, *When Buffalo Free the Mountains: The Survival of America's Ute Indians*. Garden City, NY: 1980, p. 13.

64. Quoted in Capps, *The Indians*, p. 192.

Chapter 7: Native American Last Stands

65. Quoted in Evan S. Connell, *Son of the Morning Star: Custer and the Little Bighorn*. San Francisco: North Point, 1984, p. 249.

66. Quoted in Connell, *Son of the Morning Star*, p. 238.

67. Quoted in Connell, *Son of the Morning Star*, p. 331.

68. Quoted in Connell, *Son of the Morning Star*, p. 261.

69. Quoted in Brown, *Bury My Heart at Wounded Knee*, p. 311.

70. Quoted in PBS, "Chief Joseph," *New Perspectives on the West*. www.pbs.org /weta/thewest/people/a_c/chiefjos eph.htm.

71. Quoted in Annette Rosenstiel, *Red & White: Indian Views of the White Man 1492–1982*. New York: Universe, 1983, pp. 107–108.

72. Quoted in Brown, *Bury My Heart at Wounded Knee*, p. 404.

73. Quoted in Brown, *Bury My Heart at Wounded Knee*, p. 414.

74. Quoted in Brown, *Bury My Heart at Wounded Knee*, p. 417.

75. Quoted in Jones, *Christopher Columbus and His Legacy*, pp. 116–117.

76. Quoted in Nabokov, *Native American Testimony*, p. 231.

Chapter 8: Losing Ground on the Reservations

77. Quoted in Davis, *North American Indian*, p. 96.

78. Little Rock Reed, "Broken Treaties, Broken Promises: The United States's Continuing Campaign Against Native People," *Social Issues Resources Series*, no. 68, May/June 1992, pp. 48+.

79. Janet A. McDonnell, *The Dispossession of the American Indian 1887–1934*. Bloomington: Indiana University Press, 1991, pp. 9–10.

80. Quoted in McDonnell, *The Dispossession of the American Indian 1887–1934*, pp. 31–32.

81. *Lone Wolf, Principal Chief of the Kiowas, et al., vs. Ethan A. Hitchcock, Secretary of the Interior, et al.* No. 275, Supreme

Court of the United States, Argued October 23, 1902, Decided January 5, 1903. C. Williams Rice, Associate Professor of Law, University of Tulsa College of Law. www.utulsa.edu/law/classes/rice/USSCT_Cases/Lone_Wolf_v_Hitchcock_187_553.htm.

Chapter 9: Holding On to What Is Left

82. McDonnell, *The Dispossession of the American Indian 1887–1934*, p. 4.

83. Quoted in Donald Lee Fixico, *Termination and Relocation: Federal Indian Policy in the 1950s.* Norman: University of Oklahoma Press, 1980, p. 20.

84. Quoted in Fixico, *Termination and Relocation*, p. 21.

85. Fixico, *Termination and Relocation*, pp. 7–8.

86. Quoted in Fixico, *Termination and Relocation*, p. 21.

87. Quoted in Sharon O'Brien, "Federal Indian Policies and Human Rights," *American Indian Policy in the Twentieth Century*, Vine Deloria Jr., ed. Norman: University of Oklahoma Press, 1985, p. 53.

88. Deloria, *American Indian Policy in the Twentieth Century*, p. 251.

89. Judith Nies, "Indian Lands, Black Gold," *Orion*, 2001. www.oriononline.org/pages/om/archive_om/Nies.html.

90. O'Brien, "Federal Indian Policies and Human Rights," p. 51.

For Further Reading

Books

Christopher Collier and James Lincoln Collier, *Clash of Cultures: Prehistory–1638*. New York: Marshall Cavendish, 1998. A richly illustrated book that provides details on the cultures of Europeans and Native Americans and how they clashed.

Arthur Diamond, *Smallpox and the American Indian*. San Diego: Lucent, 1991. A concise and informative history of the impact of smallpox and other diseases on Native Americans.

Mary Ellen Jones, ed., *Christopher Columbus and His Legacy: Opposing Viewpoints*. San Diego: Greenhaven, 1992. A compilation of writings on the impact of Columbus's discovery of the New World.

Lawrence C. Kelly, *Federal Indian Policy*. New York: Chelsea House, 1990. A readable overview of U.S. policy toward Native Americans from the colonial period to modern times.

Richard B. Morris, *The Indian Wars*. Minneapolis: Lerner, 1985. A concise and factual account of the conflicts between Europeans and the Five Civilized Tribes along the Atlantic coast.

Don Nardo, *The Indian Wars*. San Diego: Lucent, 1991. A dramatic account of the major wars between Native Americans and the Europeans and Americans.

Frank W. Porter III, *The Bureau of Indian Affairs*. New York: Chelsea House, 1988. A book for the general reader that traces the controversial history of the U.S. Bureau of Indian Affairs.

Russell Shorto, *Tecumseh and the Dream of an American Indian Nation*. Englewood Cliffs, NJ: Silver Burdett, 1989. An informative biography that traces the life of the great Indian leader.

Liz Sonneborn, *The New York Public Library Amazing Native American History: A Book of Answers for Kids*. New York: John Wiley, 1999. An informative and up-to-date compilation of interesting questions and answers concerning the culture and history of North American Indians.

Ray Spargenburg and Diane K. Moser, *The American Indian Experience*. New York: Facts On File, 1997. An illustrated guide for students to ruins, parks, monuments, and other historic sites relating to the history of Native Americans.

Jeanne Williams, *Trail of Tears: American Indians Driven from Their Lands*. Dallas: Hendrik-Long, 1992. A dramatic narrative history, focusing on the forcible removal of various tribes from their ancient homelands.

Web Sites

American Indians (www.42explore2.com /native.htm). A privately sponsored educational resource site for students, parents, and teachers with links to archives of Native American biographies, tribal histories, and articles on important battles, events, and movements.

American Indians and the Natural World (www.carnegiemuseums.org/cmnh/exhibits/north-south-east-west). An exhibit of the Carnegie Museum of Natural History, this site explores Native Americans' spiritual and philosophical beliefs about the natural world. The site focuses on the practical knowledge and activities of one tribe in each of the four major regions of the United States.

Digital History: Native American Voices (www.digitalhistory.uh.edu/native_voices/native_voices.cfm). A comprehensive collection of documents, primary sources, and images of Native American history, maintained by the collaborative effort of the University of Houston, Chicago Historical Society, Gilder Lehrman Institute of American History, Houston Museum of Fine Arts, and the National Parks Service, U.S. Department of the Interior.

Works Consulted

Books

Ralph K. Andrist, *The Long Death: The Last Days of the Plains Indian*. New York: Macmillan, 1964. A scholarly but readable chronicle.

Stephen Ambrose and Douglas Brinkley, eds., *Witness to America*. New York: HarperCollins, 1999. A collection of primary documents of American history.

Alan Axelrod, *Chronicle of the Indian Wars: From Colonial Times to Wounded Knee*. New York: Prentice-Hall, 1993. A lively history of the major Indian Wars.

Edward S. Barnard, ed., *Story of the Great American West*. Pleasantville, NY: Reader's Digest Association, 1977. A popular history of the West for the general reader.

John M. Blum et al., *The National Experience: A History of the United States*. 6th ed. San Diego: Harcourt Brace Jovanovich, 1985. A classic college-level history.

Daniel Boorstin, *The Americans: The Colonial Experience*. New York: Random House, 1958. An excellent history of America's colonial days, including firsthand accounts of white and Indian encounters.

———, *The Discoverers*. New York: Random House, 1983. A popular history of the world's great discoveries.

Dee Brown, *Bury My Heart at Wounded Knee*. New York: Bantam, 1970. This highly acclaimed yet controversial book painfully recounts, from the Indians' point of view, how the West was lost.

Benjamin Capps, *The Indians*. New York: Time-Life, 1973. An illustrated study of the culture and history of the Native Americans in the Old West.

Gorton Carruth, *What Happened When: A Chronology of Life and Events in America*. New York: Signet, Penguin, 1991. A useful reference book.

Oliver Perry Chitwood, *A History of Colonial America*. New York: Harper & Row, 1961. A scholarly work on America's colonial past.

Noam Chomsky, *Hegemony or Survival: America's Quest for Global Dominance*. New York: Henry Holt, 2003. A critique of American foreign policy, including discussion of U. S. dealings with American Indian tribes.

Henry Steele Commager, ed., *Documents of American History*. New York: Appleton-Century-Crofts, 1948. A comprehensive collection of essential primary sources of American history.

Alastair Cooke, *America*. New York: Knopf, 1977. A popular history.

Evan S. Connell, *Son of the Morning Star: Custer and the Little Bighorn*. San Francisco: North Point, 1984. A well-written biography of the infamous Indian fighter.

Christopher Davis, *North American Indian.* London: Hamlyn, 1969. A lyrical narrative of the conquest of Native Americans and their struggle to exist in the modern world.

Vine Deloria Jr., *Custer Died for Your Sins: An Indian Manifesto.* Norman: University of Oklahoma Press, 1969, 1988. A collection of Deloria's personal essays on Indian issues.

Vine Deloria Jr., ed., *American Indian Policy in the Twentieth Century.* Norman: University of Oklahoma Press, 1985. A collection of eleven essays written by contemporary scholars on federal Indian policies.

Mary Crow Dog, with Richard Erdoes, *Lakota Woman.* New York: Grove Weidenfeld, 1990. An intimate, first-person account of a contemporary Indian woman growing up on a reservation in South Dakota. For mature readers, this is a blunt and honest look at the radicalization of an Indian activist in the 1970s.

William Dudley, ed., *Native Americans: Opposing Viewpoints.* San Diego: Greenhaven, 1998. An anthology of essays, documents, and other publications relating the experiences of Native Americans from the arrival of Europeans to the late twentieth century.

Editors of the Reader's Digest Association, *Through Indian Eyes: The Untold Story of the American Peoples.* Pleasantville, NY: 1995. A lavishly illustrated history that emphasizes Native American daily experience through oral and personal accounts.

Executive Orders Relating to Indian Reservations, 1855–1922. Wilmington, DE: Scholarly Resources, 1975. A compilation of the original orders given by U.S. presidents and various other government officials pertaining to Indian reservations.

Eyewitnesses and Other Readings in American History. Vol. 2, *1865 to the Present.* Austin: Holt, Rinehart, and Winston, 1991. A compilation of primary sources.

Donald Lee Fixico, *Termination and Relocation: Federal Indian Policy in the 1950s.* Norman: University of Oklahoma Press, 1980. A scholarly yet readable dissertation on the federal government's attempt to dissolve Indian tribes and relocate Native Americans.

Grant Foreman, *The Five Civilized Tribes.* Norman: University of Oklahoma Press, 1934. A scholarly book based on missionary letters, government documents, and interviews with survivors of forced relocation.

Thomas Froncek, ed., *Voices from the Wilderness.* New York: McGraw-Hill, 1974. A compilation of personal accounts of America's frontiersmen in their own words from 1775 to 1870.

Geronimo, *Geronimo: His Own Story.* Ed. with an introduction and notes by Frederick W. Turner III. New York: Ballantine, 1970. A readable translation of Geronimo's oral autobiography.

Rebecca Brooks Gruver, *An American History: Vol. 1, To 1877.* Reading, MA: Addison-Wesley, 1972. A college-level history.

Helen Hunt Jackson, *A Century of Dishonor (A Sketch of the United States Government's Dealings with Some of the Indian Tribes).* Williamstown, MA: Corner House, 1973. Originally appearing in 1881, this classic indictment of U.S. Indian policy draws heavily on government documents.

Richard M. Ketchum, ed., *The American Heritage Book of the Pioneer Spirit*. New York: American Heritage, 1959. A popular history, interesting for its omissions concerning the dispossession of Indians.

Arleen Keylin and Eve Nelson, eds., *If Elected*. New York: Random House, 1976. A compilation of *New York Times* front page news reports from 1860 to 1960.

Susan Kingsbury, ed., *The Records of the Virginia Company of London*. Vol. 3. Washington, DC: GPO, 1933.

The Log of Christopher Columbus. Trans. Robert H. Fuson. Camden, ME: International Marine, 1987. A translated version of Columbus's log, illustrated with maps, illustrations, and engravings.

Thomas E. Mails, *The Cherokee People: The Story of the Cherokees from Earliest Origins to Contemporary Times*. Tulsa, OK: Council Oak, 1992. A comprehensive, scholarly yet readable, illustrated book that traces the origin and history of the Cherokee people.

George W. Manypenny, *Our Indian Wards*. New York: Da Capo, 1972. This classic work was first published in 1880. The author bases his plea for Indian policy reform on personal experience at the Bureau of Indian Affairs, where he served as commissioner from 1853 to 1857.

S.L.A. Marshall, *Crimsoned Prairie: The Indian Wars on the Great Plains*. New York: Charles Scribner's Sons, 1972. Written by a military historian, this work focuses on the battlefield tactics of the Indian Wars.

Janet A. McDonnell, *The Dispossession of the American Indian 1887–1934*. Bloomington: Indiana University Press, 1991. A concise, scholarly book that traces the disastrous impact of the federal government's allotment policy on Native Americans.

Robert William Mondy, *Pioneers and Preachers: Stories of the Old Frontier*. Chicago: Nelson-Hall, 1980. A readable and well-documented account of everyday existence on the American frontier.

Richard B. Morris and James Woodress, eds., *Voices from America's Past: Vol. 1, The Colonies and the New Nation*. New York: E.P. Dutton, 1961. A collection of primary source documents from America's colonial period.

Peter Nabokov, ed., *Native American Testimony: An Anthology of Indian and White Relations, First Encounter to Dispossession*. New York: Thomas Y. Crowell, 1978. A collection of primary sources that conveys the story of Indian and white encounters in America in the voices of American Indians.

Wilfred T. Neill, *Florida's Seminole Indians*. St. Petersburg, FL: Great Outdoors, 1956. A concise, popular history of the Seminole.

Leonard Pitt, *We Americans*. Vol. 2, *1865 to the Present*. Glenview, IL: Scott, Foresman, 1976. A college-level textbook.

Little Rock Reed, "Broken Treaties, Broken Promises: The United States's Continuing Campaign Against Native People," *Social Issues Resources Series*, no. 68, May/June 1992.

Robert V. Remini, *The Life of Andrew Jackson*. New York: Harper & Row, 1988. A condensation of a three-volume work by a renowned historian. Readable and more sympathetic to Jackson than many other biographies.

Roger RienDeau, *A Brief History of Canada*. New York: Facts On File, 2000. A popular history.

Annette Rosenstiel, *Red & White: Indian Views of the White Man 1492–1982.* New York: Universe, 1983. A collection of primary sources—documents, speeches, letters, illustrations and photographs—tracing the Indians' view of their own removal and destruction over five centuries.

Irving Stone, *Men to Match My Mountains.* New York: Doubleday, 1956. An epic retelling of the opening of the far west, mainly from the point of view of whites.

John Upton Terrell, *Land Grab: The Truth About "The Winning of the West."* New York: Dial, 1972. A highly subjective indictment of the United States for its handling of the American Indian, backed by long excerpts from official government documents.

To America and Around the World: The Logs of Christopher Columbus and Ferdinand Magellan. Boston: Branden, 1990. Columbus's logs transcribed by Las Casas. Trans. Clement S. Markham. Magellan's logs written by Antonio Pigafetta. Trans. John Pinkerton. Columbus's own words of his initial reactions upon seeing the New World.

Alexis de Tocqueville, *Democracy in America.* Trans. George Lawrence. New York: Harper & Row, 1988. This classic work by a French observer contains firsthand descriptions of the condition of the American Indians in the first half of nineteenth-century America.

Sanford Wexler, *Westward Expansion: An Eyewitness History.* New York: Facts On File, 1991. A readable narrative and a fascinating compilation of primary sources, expressing a wide range of views of those who witnessed the westward expansion, victors and victims alike.

Gary Wills, *Under God: Religion and American Politics.* New York: Simon and Schuster, 1990. This book for the mature reader analyzes the mingling of religion and politics in American history.

Nancy Wood, *When Buffalo Free the Mountains: The Survival of America's Ute Indians.* Garden City, NY: 1980. Though this book's coverage of the contemporary problems of the Utes is dated, the sections on the tribe's history are still valuable.

Howard Zinn, *A People's History of the United States.* New York: Harper & Row, 1980. This opinionated popular history for the general reader relies heavily on primary sources and quotations to document patterns of exploitation.

Internet Sources

Lone Wolf, Principal Chief of the Kiowas, et al., vs. Ethan A. Hitchcock, Secretary of the Interior, et al. No. 275, Supreme Court of the United States, Argued October 23, 1902, Decided January 5, 1903. C. Williams Rice, Associate Professor of Law, University of Tulsa College of Law. www.utulsa.edu /law/classes/rice/USSCT_Cases/Lone _Wolf_v_Hitchcock_187_553.htm.

Judith Nies, "Indian Lands, Black Gold," *Orion,* 2001. www.oriononline.org/pages /om/archive_om/Nies.html.

PBS, "Chief Joseph," *New Perspectives on the West.* www.pbs.org/weta/thewest/ people/a_c/chiefjoseph.htm.

"Treaty with the Delawares: 1778," Avalon Project at Yale School. www.yale.edu/ lawweb/avalon/ntreaty/del1778.htm.

Index

Soviet Union, 88
Spain/Spanish, 11–15, 17, 22, 28, 40, 46
speculators, 40, 58
squatters, 31, 40, 45
standard of living, 91–92
Stanton, Edward, 67
starvation. *See* food, shortages of
suicide rate, 91
supplies, 55, 65–66
    shortages of, 42, 59, 61, 78
surplus land, 80–86
Sweden, 13

Taos Pueblo, 92
Tecumseh, 32–37
Tennessee, 38, 41
termination, policy of, 88–92
Teton Sioux, 64
Texas, 53, 67
Third Colorado Volunteers, 64
Tippecanoe Creek, 35
Tocqueville, Alexis de, 41
traders, 12, 59
Trail of Tears, 43–44, 51
trappers, 31, 52
treaties, 22, 42–43, 45–47, 54–56, 66, 77, 90
    with England, 19–20, 25–27
    violations of, 28–38, 57–58, 62, 68, 85, 88, 95
    see also non-treaty tribes; and specific treaties
Treaty of Camp Moultrie, 46–47
Treaty of Dancing Rabbit Creek, 42
Treaty of Greenville, 31, 34
Treaty of Paris, 22
tribes, 8, 10, 19
    authority of, 25, 38, 40, 43, 77–81, 86–89, 92–93
    see also non-treaty tribes; and individual tribes
trust status, 29, 81–82, 85, 89–90

United States
    boundaries of, 20, 28, 53
    land confiscation by, 28–30, 35–37
    peacekeeping by, 53, 55–56
    removal policy of, 38–48
    treatment of Native Americans by, 27–37,
        40–48, 53, 58–79, 62, 92–93
uprisings. *See* wars
urban areas. See cities, relocation to
U.S. Army, 44–48, 53–54, 58–60, 67–68, 71–75, 87
U.S. Congress, 30, 59, 61–62, 95
    legislation by, 41–42, 51, 56, 77–82, 85–89, 91–93

U.S. Forest Service, 95
U.S. Senate, 55
U.S. Supreme Court, 43, 85, 93–94
Utah Territory, 52
Ute, 66, 73

Van Buren, Martin, 44
Vattel, Emmerich von, 19
vigilantes, 68
villages, 8, 38, 51
violence, 10, 19, 43
Virginia, 20, 24–25

Wampanoag, 16–17, 94
War of 1812, 35–37
warriors, 15, 24, 30–31, 35, 54, 71, 81
wars, 8, 15–27, 31, 44–48, 54, 59–67
    see also specific wars
Washington (state), 56
Washington, George, 23, 31
Washita River, 66–68
water, 10, 81, 95
Watt, James, 95
Wea, 56
Weasel Bear, Louise, 75
Webster, L.B., 46
West, 59–68, 73–74, 77
    expansion into, 21, 25–26, 32, 37–38, 47–58, 86
West Virginia, 26
Whipple, H.B., 66–67
White Antelope, 63–64
whites
    encroachment by, 8–24, 68, 76, 80, 83–86, 89
    in Indian Territory, 47–48, 50–60, 62–65, 68
    revenge against, 24–25, 59–60, 63–64, 66–67,
        72–74
    treatment of Native Americans by, 10–23,
        27–38, 40–49, 53, 58–79, 92–95
Willamette Valley, 52
Winthrop, John, 17
Wisconsin, 34, 47–48
World War II, 87–88
Wounded Knee Creek, massacre at, 74–75
Wovoka, 74
Wyandot, 24
Wyatt, Francis, 15
Wyoming, 32, 53, 64, 66, 69, 72

Yellow Hair. *See* Custer, George Armstrong
Yellow Medicine River, 59

Picture Credits

About the Author

John M. Dunn is a freelance writer and high school history teacher. He has taught in Georgia, Florida, North Carolina, and Germany. As a writer and journalist, he has published numerous articles and stories in more than twenty periodicals, as well as scripts for audio-visual productions and a children's play. His books *The Russian Revolution, The Spread of Islam, Advertising, The Civil Rights Movement, The Enlightenment, Life During the Black Death, The Vietnam War: A History of U.S. Involvement, The Computer Revolution, The French Revolution: The Fall of the Monarchy*, and *Castro's Cuba* are published by Lucent Books. He lives with his wife and two daughters in Ocala, Florida.